D0210883

HOW AN
ECONOMY
GROWS
AND WHY IT
CRASHES

HOW AN ECONOMY GROWS

AND WHY IT CRASHES

A TALE BY

PETER D. SCHIFF

AND **ANDREW J. SCHIFF**

Illustrations by Brendan Leach

WILEY

John Wiley & Sons, Inc

Published by John Wiley & Sons, Inc., Hoboken, New Jersey.

Published simultaneously in Canada.

Based on Irwin Schiff's book, *How an Economy Grows and Why It Doesn't*, which was published by Freedom Books in 1985.

For general information on our other products and services or for technical support, please contact our Customer Care Department within the United States at (800) 762-2974, outside the United States at (317) 572-3993 or fax (317) 572-4002.

Wiley also publishes its books in a variety of electronic formats. Some content that appears in print may not be available in electronic books. For more information about Wiley products, visit our web site at www.wiley.com.

Library of Congress Cataloging-in-Publication Data:

ISBN 978-0-470-52670-5

Printed in the United States of America

10 9 8 7 6 5 4 3 2 1

To my father Irwin Schiff and fathers everywhere who tell stories to their sons, and to my son Spencer and sons everywhere who pass them on to subsequent generations.

— Peter

To Irwin for the logic, Ellen for the care and support, Ethan for the enthusiasm, Eliza for the wonder, and Paxton for the home (maybe one day we'll get the hearth).

— Andrew

CONTENTS

DISCLOSURE

In addition to being the president, Peter Schiff is also a registered representative and owner of Euro Pacific Capital, Inc. (Euro Pacific). In addition to his duties as director of communications, Andrew Schiff is also a stock broker at the firm. Euro Pacific is a FINRA registered Broker-Dealer and a member of the Securities Investor Protection Corporation (SIPC). This book has been prepared solely for informational purposes, and it is not an offer to buy or sell, or a solicitation to buy or sell, any security or instrument, or to participate in any particular trading strategy.

AUTHOR'S NOTE

In this allegory of U.S. economic history the reader will encounter many recognizable personalities and events. But as a very broad brush was needed to condense such a complex story into a cartoon book, many details have been blended.

In addition to the exploits of specific historical figures, characters represent broader ideas. For instance, while Ben Barnacle is clearly our version of Fed Chairman Ben Bernanke, Barnacle's actions in the story are not meant to solely apply to Bernanke himself. Rather, he is a representative of all highly inflationary economists.

In real life, Federal Reserve Notes were introduced 20 years before the election of Franklin D. Roosevelt. But given his penchant for spending, we decided to credit him with the innovation. And although Chris Dodd was but a child when Fannie Mae was actually created, his support of the agency in later years gives him originator status in our story. And, although the foreign islands in the book roughly correspond with actual countries, they are also stand-ins for all nations.

We ask that you forgive us these, and other, liberties of chronology and biography.

INTRODUCTION

Over the past century or so, academics have presented mankind with spectacular scientific advancements in just about all fields of study...except one.

Armed with a mastery of mathematics and physics, scientists sent a spacecraft hundreds of millions of miles to parachute to the surface of one of Saturn's moons. But the practitioners of the "dismal" science of economics can't point to a similar record of achievement.

If NASA engineers had evidenced the same level of forecasting skill as our top economists, the Galileo mission would have had a very different outcome. Not only would the satellite have missed its orbit of Saturn, but in all likelihood the rocket would have turned downward on lift-off, bored though the Earth's crust, and exploded somewhere deep in the magma.

In 2007 when the world was staring into the teeth of the biggest economic catastrophe in three generations, very few economists had any idea that there was any trouble lurking on the horizon. Three years into the mess, economists now offer remedies that strike most people as frankly ridiculous. We are told that we must go deeper into debt to fix our debt crisis, and that we must spend in order prosper. The reason their vision was so poor then, and their solutions so counterintuitive now, is that few have any idea how their science actually works.

The disconnect results from the nearly universal acceptance of the theories of John Maynard Keynes, a very smart early-twentieth century English academic who developed some very stupid ideas about what makes economies grow. Essentially Keynes managed to pull off one the neatest tricks imaginable: he made something simple seem to be hopelessly complex.

In Keynes's time, physicists were first grappling with the concept of quantum mechanics, which, among other things, imagined a cosmos governed by two entirely different sets of physical laws: one for very small particles, like protons and electrons, and another for everything else. Perhaps sensing that the boring study of economics needed a fresh shot in the arm, Keynes proposed a similar world view in which one set of economic laws came in to play at the micro level (concerning the realm of individuals and families) and another set at the macro level (concerning nations and governments).

Keynes's work came at the tail end of the most expansive economic period in the history of the world. Economically speaking, the nineteenth an early-twentieth-century produced unprecedented growth of productive capacity and living standards in the Western world. The epicenter of this boom was the freewheeling capitalism of the United States, a country unique in its preference for individual rights and limited government.

But the decentralizing elements inherent in free market capitalism threatened the rigid power structures still in place throughout much of the world. In addition, capitalistic expansion did come with some visible extremes of wealth and poverty, causing some social scientists and progressives to seek what they believed was a more equitable alternative to free market capitalism. In his quest to bring the guidance of modern science to the seemingly unfair marketplace, Keynes unwittingly gave cover to central authorities and social utopians who believed that economic activity needed to be planned from above.

At the core of his view was the idea that governments could smooth out the volatility of free markets by expanding the supply of money and running large budget deficits when times were tough.

When they first burst onto the scene in the 1920s and 1930s, the disciples of Keynes (called Keynesians), came into conflict with the "Austrian School" which followed the views of economists such as Ludwig von Mises. The Austrians argued that recessions are necessary to compensate for unwise decisions made during the booms that always precede the bursts. Austrians believe that the booms are created in the first place by the false signals sent to businesses when government's "stimulate" economies with low interest rates.

So whereas the Keynesians look to mitigate the busts, Austrians look to prevent artificial booms.

In the economic showdown that followed, the Keynesians had a key advantage.

Because it offers the hope of pain-free solutions, Keynesianism was an instant hit with politicians. By promising to increase employment and boost growth without raising taxes or cutting government services, the policies advocated by Keynes were the economic equivalent of miracle weight-loss programs that required no dieting or exercise. While irrational, such hopes are nevertheless soothing, and are a definite attraction on the campaign trail.

Keynesianism permits governments to pretend that they have the power to raise living standards with the whir of a printing press.

As a consequence of their pro-government bias, Keynesians were much more likely than Austrians to receive the highest government economic appointments. Universities that produced finance ministers and Treasury secretaries obviously acquired more prestige than universities that could not. Inevitably economics departments began to favor professors who supported those ideas. Austrians were increasingly relegated to the margins.

Similarly, large financial institutions, the other major employers of economists, have an equal affinity for Keynesian dogma. Large banks and investment firms are more profitable in the Keynesian environment of easy money and loose credit. The belief that government policy should backstop investments also helps financial firms pry open the pocketbooks of skittish investors. As a result, they are more likely to hire those economists who support such a worldview.

With such glaring advantages over their stuffy rivals, a self-fulfilling mutual admiration society soon produced a corps of top economists inbred with a loyalty to Keynesian principles.

These analysts take it as gospel that Keynesian policies were responsible for ending the Great Depression. Many have argued that without the stimuli provided by government (including expenditures necessary to wage the Second World War), we would never have recovered from the economic abyss. Absent from this analysis is the fact that the Depression was the longest and most severe downturn in modern history and the first that was ever dealt with using the full range of Keynesian policy tools. Whether these interventions were the cause or the cure of the Depression is apparently a debate that no serious "economist" ever thought was worth having.

With Keynesians in firm control of economics departments, financial ministries, and investment banks, it's as if we have entrusted astrologers instead of astronomers to calculate orbital velocities of celestial bodies. (Yes, the satellite crashed into an asteroid, but it is an unexpected encounter that could lead to enticing possibilities!)

The tragi-comic aspect of the situation is that no matter how often these economists completely flub their missions, no matter how many rockets explode on the launchpad, no one of consequence ever questions their models.

Most ordinary people have come to justifiably feel that economists don't know what they are talking about. But most assume that they are clueless because the field itself is so vast,

vast, murky, and illogical that true predictive power is beyond even the best and most educated minds.

But what if I told you that the economic duality proposed by the Keynesians doesn't exist? What if economics is much simpler than that? What if what is good for the goose is good for the gander? What if it were equally impossible for a family, or a nation, to spend its way to prosperity?

Many people who are familiar with my accurate forecasting of the economic crash of 2008 like to credit my intelligence as the source of my vision. I can assure you that I am no smarter than most of the economists who couldn't see an asset bubble if it spent a month in their living room. What I do have is a solid and fundamental understanding of the basic principles of economics.

I have that advantage because as a child my father provided me with the basic tool kit I needed to cut through the economic clutter. The tools came to me in the form of stories, allegories, and thought experiments. One of those stories serves as the basis for this book.

Irwin Schiff has become a figure of some renown and is most associated with the national movement to resist the federal income tax. For more than 35 years he has challenged, often obsessively, the methods of the Internal Revenue Service while maintaining that the income tax is enforced in violation of the Constitution's three taxing clauses, the 16th Amendment, and the revenue laws themselves. He has written many books on the subject and has openly challenged the federal government in court. For these activities, he continues to pay a heavy personal price. At 82 he remains incarcerated in federal prison.

But before he turned his attention to taxes, Irwin Schiff made a name for himself as an economist.

He was born in 1928 in New Haven, Connecticut, the eighth child of a lower-middle-class immigrant family. His father was a union man, and his entire extended family enthusiastically supported Roosevelt's New Deal. When he entered the University of Connecticut in 1946 to study economics, nothing in his background or temperament would have led anyone to believe that he would reject the dominant orthodoxy, and to instead embrace the economic views espoused by the out-of-fashion Austrians...but he did.

Irwin always had the power of original thinking, which, combined with a rather outsized belief in himself, perhaps led him to sense that the lessons he was learning did not fully mesh with reality. Digging deeper into the full spectrum of economic theory, Irwin came across books by libertarian thinkers like Henry Hazlitt and Henry Grady Weaver. Although his conversion was gradual (taking the full decade of the 1950's to complete), he eventually emerged as a full-blooded believer in sound money, limited government, low taxes, and personal responsibility. By 1964, Irwin enthusiastically supported Barry Goldwater for president.

At the 1944 Bretton Woods Monetary Conference, the United States persuaded the nations of the world to back their currencies with dollars instead of gold. Since the United States pledged to exchange an ounce of gold for every 35 dollars, and it owned 80 percent of the world's gold, the arrangement was widely accepted.

However, 40 years of monetary inflation brought about by Keynesian money managers at the Federal Reserve caused the pegged price of gold to be severely undervalued. This mismatch led to what became known as the "gold drain," a mass run by foreign governments, led by France in 1965, to redeem U.S. Federal Reserve Notes for gold. Given the opportunity to buy gold at the old 1932 price, foreign governments were quickly depleting U.S. reserves.

In 1968, President Lyndon Johnson's economic advisors argued that the gold drain resulted not from the attraction of bargain basement prices, but because foreign governments feared that U.S. gold reserves were insufficient to provide backing for domestically held notes *and* to redeem foreign notes. To dispel this anxiety, the president's monetary experts advised him to remove the required 25 percent gold backing from domestic dollars so that these reserves would be available for foreign dollar holders. Presumably this added protection would assuage the concerns of foreign governments and would stop the gold hemorrhage. Irwin, then a young business owner in New Haven, Connecticut, thought their reasoning was absurd.

Irwin sent a letter to Texas Senator John Tower, who was then a member of the committee reviewing the gold issue, explaining that the United States faced two choices: force down the general price structure to bring it in line with the 1932 price of gold, or raise gold to bring it in line with 1968 prices. In other words, to adjust for 40 years of Keynesian inflation, America now had to either deflate prices or devalue the dollar.

Although Irwin argued that deflation would be the most responsible course, since it would restore the lost purchasing power of the dollar, he understood that economists erroneously view falling prices as a catastrophe and that governments have a natural preference for inflation (as will be explored in this book). Given these biases, he argued that authorities could at least acknowledge prior debasement and officially devalue the dollar against gold. In such a scenario, he felt that gold would have to be priced at $105 per ounce.

He also feared a much more likely, and dangerous, third option: that the government would do nothing (which was precisely what they chose to do). Then as now, the choice was between facing the music or deferring the problem to future generations. They deferred, and we are the future generation.

Tower was so impressed with the basic logic of his arguments, that he invited Irwin in to address the entire committee. At the hearings, all the highly placed monetary experts from the Federal Reserve, the Treasury Department, and Congress testified that removing gold backing would strengthen the dollar, cause the price of gold to fall, and usher in an age of prosperity.

In his testimony, Irwin asserted that the removal of gold backing from U.S. currency would cause gold prices to soar. But more importantly, he warned that a currency devoid of any intrinsic value would lead to massive inflation and unsustainable government debt. This minority opinion was completely ignored, and gold backing was removed.*

Contrary to everything the economists had predicted, the availability of additional reserves failed to stop the outflows of gold. Finally, in 1971 President Richard Nixon closed the window, which severed the dollar's last link to gold. At that point, the global economic system became completely based on worthless money. Over the next decade, the United States experienced the nastiest outbreak of inflation in our history and gold headed towards $800 per ounce.

In 1972 Irwin set out to write his first major attack on how Keynesian economics was putting the United States on an unsustainable economic course. His book *The Biggest Con: How the Government Is Fleecing You*, enjoyed wide-spread critical acclaim and decent sales. Among the many anecdotes the book contained was a story about three men on an island who fished with their hands.

The story had its genesis as a simple time killer on family car trips. When caught in traffic, Irwin attempted to entertain his two young sons with basic lessons of economics (any boy's idea of a perfect afternoon). To do this he almost always resorted to funny stories. This one became known as "The Fish Story."

The allegory served as the centerpiece of a chapter in *The Biggest Con*. About eight years later, after so many readers had commented to him about how much they loved the

* To read Irwin's complete testimony, please see Appendix A of *The Biggest Con: How the Government Is Fleecing You*, (Freedom Books, 1978).

story, he decided to develop an entire illustrated book around it. *How an Economy Grows and Why It Doesn't* was first published in 1979, and went on to achieve quasi-cult status among devotees of Austrian economics.

Thirty years later, as I watched the United States' economy head off a cliff, and as I watched our government repeating and redoubling the mistakes of the past, my brother and I thought it would be an ideal time to revise and update "The Fish Story" for a new generation.

Certainly, there has never been a greater need for a dose of economic clarity, and the story is the best tool we know of to give people a better understanding of what makes our economy tick.

This version is in many ways more ambitious than the one Irwin drafted 30 years ago. Our scope is wider, and our attempt to incorporate the historical sequence is deeper. In fact, the story would best be described as a riff on the original.

We hope that the book can appeal to the kind of people who typically go numb when they hear economists drone on about concepts that seem to have nothing to do with reality. We intend to show that the model proposed by the Keynesians, whereby governments can spend without consequence in the belief that worthless money can be an effective economic lubricant, is false and dangerous.

The bad news is that when you take off the rose-colored glasses that all of our economists have forgotten they are wearing, you can see clearly that our nation is confronting serious problems that we are currently making worse, not better. The good news is that if we allow ourselves some clarity, then we can at least make an attempt to solve the problems.

And while the subject matter is deadly serious, we approached the project with the kind of humor that is absolutely vital in times of stress—just as Irwin would have wanted it.

CHAPTER
1
AN IDEA
IS BORN

Once upon a time there were three men—Able, Baker, and Charlie—who lived alone on an island. Far from a tropical paradise, the island was a rough place with no luxuries. In particular, food options were extremely limited. The menu consisted of just one item: fish.

Fortunately, the island was surrounded by an abundant
population of strangely homogeneous fish, any one of
which was large enough to feed one human being for one
day. However, this was
an isolated place where
none of mankind's many
advancements in fish-catching
technology had arrived. The
best these guys could do was
jump in and grab the slimy
buggers by hand.

Using this inefficient technique, each could catch one
fish per day, which was just enough to survive to the next
day. This activity amounted to the sum total of their island
economy. Wake, fish, eat, sleep. Not much of a life, but hey,
it beats the alternative.

And so, in this super-
simple, sushi-based
island society
there are....

No savings!

No credit!

No investment!

Everything that is produced is consumed! There is nothing
saved for a rainy day, and there is nothing left to lend.

Although our island dwellers lived in a primitive society, it didn't mean that they were stupid or lacked ambition. Like all humans, Able, Baker, and Charlie wanted to improve their living standards. But in order to do this, they had to be able to catch more than one fish apiece per day, which was the minimum they needed to survive. Unfortunately, given the limitations of their bare hands and the agility of fish, the three were stuck at subsistence level.

One night, looking up into the star-studded sky, Able began pondering the meaning of his life…. "Is this all there is? There must be more to life than **this**."

You see, Able wanted to do something besides fishing by hand. He'd love to make some better, more fashion-forward palm-leaf clothing, he wanted a place to shelter himself from monsoons, and ultimately, of course, he wanted to direct feature films. But with his daily toil so devoted to fishing, how could these dreams ever come true?

His mental wheels started turning… and suddenly an idea for a **fish catcher** was born…a device that could vastly expand the reach of the human hand while severely reducing a fish's ability to escape after the initial grab. With such a contraption, perhaps more fish could be caught in less time! With his newfound time, perhaps he could start to make better clothes, build a shelter, and put the finishing touches on his screenplay.

As the device took shape in his mind, the orchestral music began to swell, and suddenly he conceived of a future free from daily fish drudgery.

He decided to call his device a "net," and he set about finding materials to build one.

The next day, Baker and Charlie noticed that Able wasn't fishing. Instead, he was standing in the sand, making string out of palm bark. "What gives?" asked Baker. "Are you on a diet or something? If you keep sitting there tying those strings, you're gonna go hungry."

Able explained, "I have been inspired to create a device that will unlock oceans of fishing possibilities. When I'm finished, I'll spend less time fishing, and I'll never go hungry again."

Charlie rolled his eyes and wondered if his friend had finally lost his mind. "This is madness, I tell you... madness. When it doesn't work, don't come crying for a piece of my fish. Just because I'm sane doesn't mean I'm gonna pay for your crazy."

Undeterred, Able continued weaving.

✔ REALITY CHECK

In this simple task, Able is demonstrating a basic economic principle that can lead to an improvement in living standards: He is **underconsuming** and he is taking **risk!**

Underconsumption: In order to build his net, Able is unable to fish that day. He has to forgo the income (the fish) that he would have otherwise caught and eaten. It's not that Able lacks the demand for fish. In fact, he loves fish and he will go hungry if he doesn't get one that day. Able has no more or less demand for fish than his two friends. But he is choosing to defer that consumption in order to potentially consume more in the future.

Risktaking: Able is also taking risk because he has no idea that his device will actually work, or allow him to catch enough fish to compensate for his sacrifice. In the end, he might just have a bunch of string and an empty stomach. If his idea fails, he can expect no compensation from Baker and Charlie, who did, after all, try to warn him of his folly.

In economic terms, capital is a piece of equipment that is built and used not for its own sake, but for building or making something else that is wanted. Able doesn't want the net. He wants the fish. The net can, maybe, get him more fish. Therefore, the net, a piece of capital, is valuable.

By day's end Able had completed his net! He had **created capital** through his **self-sacrifice!**

That night, while Baker and Charlie slept with full stomachs, Able dealt with hunger pangs while images of luscious fish danced in his head. However, his pain was more than overcome by his hope that he had done the right thing and that a bright, fish-filled future awaited.

The next day, Baker and Charlie made much sport of Able's invention.

"Hey, that's quite a nice-looking hat," said Baker.

"A little hot for tennis, don't ya think?" added Charlie.

"Laugh it up, boys," responded Able, "but let's see who's laughing when I'm up to my armpits in fish guts."

As Able charged into the surf, the ridicule kept coming as he awkwardly handled his strange new device.

After a few minutes he got the hang of it and in no time snagged a doozy.

Baker and Charlie stopped laughing. When, in just another hour, Able landed his second fish of the day, the boys were in awe. After all, it generally took them all day to get just one fish!

From this one simple act, the island's economy was about to change in a very big way. Able had just increased his productivity, and that was a good thing for everybody.

For the moment, Able pondered his sudden boon. "Since I can provide two days of food with only one day of fishing, I can use every other day to do something else. The possibilities are endless!"

✔ REALITY CHECK

By doubling his **productivity** Able is now able to produce more than he needs to consume. From gains in productivity all other economic benefits flow.

Before Able rolled the dice to build his net, the island had no store of savings. His willingness to take a chance and go hungry led to the island's first piece of capital equipment, which in turn produced savings (for the sake of this story we will assume that fish do not spoil). This spare production is the lifeblood of a healthy economy.

TAKEAWAY

For all species, except our own, economics really boils down to day-to-day survival. Given the competition for scarce food, the harshness of the elements, the danger of predators, the vulnerability to disease, and the relative rarity of innovation, bare-bones survival (with some time left over for reproduction) is about all animals can attain. We would be in the same boat (as we were in the not-too-distant past) if not for two things: our big brains and our dexterous hands. Using the two together, we have been able to build tools and machines that magnify our ability to get more out of our environment.

Economist Thomas Woods likes to challenge his students with a simple thought experiment: What kind of economy would we have if all machines and tools disappeared? Cars, tractors, iron smelters, shovels, wheelbarrows, saws, hammers, spears, everything. What if they all went *poof* and all that we consumed had to be hunted, gathered, grown, and made, WITH OUR BARE HANDS?

Without question, life would be rough. Imagine how hard it would be to eat if we had to bring down game with our teeth, fists, and fingernails. Large game would be out of the question. Rabbits would be within our power to subdue… but you would have to catch them first. What if vegetables had to be planted and picked by hand, and what if we didn't even have sacks in which to carry the harvest? Imagine if we had to make clothes and furniture without factories… without even scissors or nails?

Despite our intelligence, we would be no better off, economically at least, than chimps and orangutans.

Tools change everything and create the possibility of an economy. Spears help us bring down game, shovels help us plant crops, and nets help us catch fish. These devices magnify the efficacy of our labor. The more we can make, the more we can consume, and the more prosperous our lives become.

The simplest definition of *economy* is the effort to maximize the availability of limited resources (and just about every resource is limited) to meet as many human demands as possible. Tools, capital, and innovation are the keys to this equation.

Keeping this in mind, it is easy to see what makes economies grow: finding better ways of producing more stuff that humans want. This doesn't change…no matter how big an economy eventually gets.

CHAPTER
2
SHARING THE WEALTH

Able, the entrepreneur, seems to have a bright future. But what about the rest of the island? Haven't we just created a caste system of the have and have-nots? Will Baker and Charlie suffer because of Able's success? Not likely. Although it was never his intention to benefit anyone other than himself, Able's capital helps everyone nevertheless. Let's see how.

After witnessing the ease with which Able now catches his fish, Baker and Charlie asked him to share his innovative fish catcher.

"Hey, Able," said Charlie, "since you use that thingy only every other day, how about you let me use it the day you're out doing other stuff?"

"C'mon, share the wealth, buddy," added Baker.

But Able didn't just fall off the tuna truck yesterday. He remembers his self-sacrifice…he remembered their scorn, and he thought of the risk. "What if they break my net? What if they just don't give it back? Then it's back to square one for me. So long, designer leafwear!"

With all this downside, Able turned them down. "Sorry, guys, no can do. I made my own net, so can you. At least you guys know that the thing works!"

Although Charlie saw the efficiency of using a net, he was apprehensive about the prospect of building one for himself.

He responded to Able, "How do I know if I'll get it right? I've never made one of those things before, and besides I don't do well with hunger. I get the shakes. I might starve to death before I make a decent net!"

Baker stepped forward with another proposal. "Okay tightwad, so you're not gonna do us any favors. We get it. But how about this? Lend us some of your surplus fish to eat while we make our own nets. That way we won't starve as we build, and we'll repay every fish we borrow from you from the extra fish we catch!"

Although the idea appealed to Able more than giving away his net, he was still very skeptical. "But if I lend you my fish, I have no guarantee that you won't just lie on the beach and take the 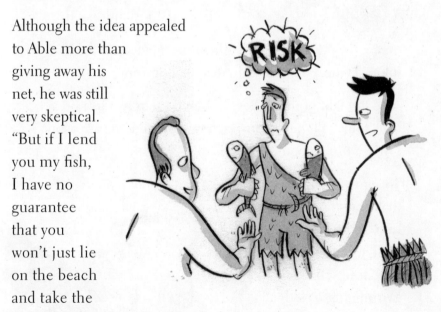 day off! Even if you build your own nets, they may not even work. Either way, you'll never be able to repay me, and I would have lost my savings for nothing! You gotta do better than that."

Charlie and Baker conceded the point. They realized that they were asking Able to take a risk for no personal benefit. But the lure of extra fish was too strong. Before long they came up with a way to entice him into taking a chance.

They thought, they crunched the numbers, and finally a **financial idea** was born!

Baker approached Able and said, "Let's make a deal: For every fish you lend us, we'll pay you back two. That's a 100 percent profit. Where else are you gonna get a return like that on an island like this?"

Able is persuaded, "Now *that* **interests** me!" he said with no apparent irony.

Able thought of the riches, "If I lend them **two** fish I'll get back **four**." I'll be two fish richer without doing any work. I'll be a fish tycoon!"

To some it may appear that Able has crossed a line. If this were a Hollywood movie he would start twirling his waxed mustache. He would be making money off the backs of others' labor, drawing profits from their toil!

But that image doesn't hold water. Even if Able intends only to fill his own fish coffers, his greed, for lack of a better word, would provide a benefit that would have otherwise been unavailable.

It's important to note that Able does not need to make the loan. He has other options, including these four:

1. He simply might hold on to his fish for future use....This is the most secure option. He would be guaranteed to not have any losses, but of course his savings *wouldn't grow*.

2. He could simply indulge himself and **consume** his savings.

3. He could build his own net rental company. He reckoned that if he consumed one of his reserve fish a day for two days, he could build two more nets.

He could then rent the extra nets to Baker and Charlie for half of a fish each day. With each of the two kicking in half of a fish every day to his net rental company, Able would have the one fish a day he needs to live, without ever having to go fishing himself. Hello, early retirement!

In this scenario, Baker and Charlie would be able to catch two fish per day with their new nets. After paying Able their half fish rent per day, they would still have one and a half fish per day each. That's 50 percent more than they would have had with no nets. It's a win-win.

Although intriguing, Able noticed some flaws in his logic. Baker and Charlie might rent the nets for two days… then use their savings to build nets for themselves. In such a scenario he would be only two fish ahead…that's a real risk!

4. He could lend out his two fish to Baker and Charlie and charge them 100 percent interest. In this scenario, he'd get four fish back if they paid him back in full with interest. But, there was always a risk that they'd stiff him.

Decisions…decisions…decisions!

To summarize, Able (and society) can do only five things with savings:

1. He can save what he has saved.

2. He can consume what he has saved.

3. He can lend out what he has saved.

4. He can invest what he has saved.

5. He can try a combination of the other four options.

Unquestionably, Able's ultimate decision will be based on his own desire for risk and reward. But whatever he does, he is benefiting the island economy and is imposing no burdens on his neighbors.

In the end, Able decides to make the loan.

✔ REALITY CHECK

As a result of Able's willingness, and ability, to make loans, Baker and Charlie now have nets that they didn't own before. With nets available to all, the island's collective fishing capacity has been raised from three fish per day to six. The economy has doubled in size, and the future looks brighter.

But this didn't happen just because the three guys were unsatisfied with their limited lifestyle. Their hunger, which is labeled "demand" in economic terms, was necessary to spur economic growth but not sufficient to achieve it.

Demand for more is natural to all humans. No matter what we have, we always want more. Maybe not more stuff, but certainly more time, more fun, and more choices, all of which requires more capital. Able, Baker, and Charlie likely had the same fish gripes for years. The difference is that they were finally able to expand productivity to meet those demands.

With their extra fish, the islanders can finally eat more than one fish per day. But the economy didn't grow because they consumed more. **They consumed more because the economy grew.** This is a simple concept, but it's amazing what modern economists can do with a simple concept.

Most economists think that demand can be increased by giving people more money to spend. But that doesn't change real demand, just how much people can spend on items that have been produced. Only by increasing supply can people actually get more of what they demand.

To some it may appear that Able used his advantage to exploit his needy neighbors. And while it's true that he made a profit without working, it doesn't mean he gets something for nothing. Able's profit is his compensation for the risks he takes. What's more, his ability to profit doesn't hinder the advancement of his peers.

Because of Able's desire to make a profit from his savings, Baker and Charlie got the opportunity to build nets without having to under consume. If they succeed, they will have improved their economic futures without having to go hungry. The rest will be gravy…or more accurately, fish oil. At that point, they themselves will have excess capital. If they fail, and are unable to pay back the loan, it's Able who takes the loss.

Essentially, the lender can benefit only if the borrower benefits.

Of course, others may not see the mutual benefits as clearly. What if, upon seeing Able's sudden expansion of wealth, Baker and Charlie grew envious and demanded a portion of his savings?

Imagine this alternative scenario:

Baker fretted, "Look at that guy lording it over us with his fancy palm-leaf tuxedo, while we sweat it out in the waves every day wrangling slimy fish. Hasn't that guy ever heard of charity? Couldn't he just spare me a fish or two so I could take a day off once in a while? He's got so many fish piling up, he'd never even know one was gone."

Charlie concurred, "Share the wealth, elitist!"

Or, what about this scenario:

Let's suppose Able, feeling somewhat guilty about his comparative wealth, was swayed by their arguments and gave away his fish, asking for nothing in return. What would Baker and Charlie do with the extra fish?

If they were free from the burden of repayment, they would most likely use the gift to increase their leisure time. And while there is nothing inherently wrong with leisure (in fact, it is the goal of most human activity), Baker and Charlie's vacation would not increase the island's productive capacity by a herring. And so while the charity option sounds more magnanimous, and may improve Able's popularity, it doesn't provide the economic boost that a business loan would.

The bottom line is that anything that leads to more fish catching (production) benefits the island. The more fish there are, the more possibilities there are for everybody to eat more, do something besides fishing, or perhaps, do nothing at all.

✔ REALITY CHECK

Some may wonder what would happen if Able turns out to be a really greedy guy, who would use his new wealth just to get richer and richer.

Is this really a danger? If the only way to make his savings grow (without working himself) is to make it available to other members of the community, why would he hoard it?

Otherwise his wealth will stay the same or get smaller as he personally consumes it! The best thing about private capitalism is that it forces those who may only be motivated by personal gain to raise the living standards of others.

TAKEAWAY

Wealth is always a relative term. In a primitive society where little is produced, even the richest can't match the material well-being available to the poor of an industrialized economy. In the Middle Ages, even the mightiest kings lacked the basic amenities that nearly everyone in the United States now takes for granted… things like central heating, indoor plumbing, and fresh vegetables in the winter. And although Baker and Charlie would imagine that a two-fish-per-day diet was the height of luxury, from our perspective such a lifestyle hardly seems enviable.

But the fact that there are degrees of wealth has always struck some as being inherently unfair. Central in this unease is the belief that the rich become that way because they take wealth from others, thereby creating the poor. In modern economics, some have even labeled this idea "the labor theory of value," which states that profit is created by paying workers less than they are worth. In this view, entrepreneurs, like Able or giant corporations for that matter, can get rich only if they succeed in making others poor.

This idea has everything to do with moral posturing, and nothing to do with reality. The reason that the rich get that way (at least initially) is that they offer something of value to others. Able offers loans to those who have inadequate savings. If he profits, it's only because the service he provides is valuable to others.

If Able were a big bully and could simply steal half of his neighbors' catch every day, then it would be true that his relative wealth would be derived from the relative poverty of those he oppresses. But these actions, which would involve forcing others to do something against their own interests, would not increase the island's overall productive capacity. He would simply take what others have produced, and the island's production would remain the same. More likely, overall capacity would fall. The oppressed would cut back on their work when they realized the fruits of their labor would be stolen.

Large-scale examples of such coercion dominate history. Slavery, serfdom, and peasantry all come to mind. And while workers do respond to force when their self-interest is denied, they respond far better if they are the beneficiaries of their labor.

Unfortunately, examples of large-scale economic freedom are rare in global history. But when self-interest is allowed to flourish, productive capacity expands quickly.

The use of credit is the perfect example of how economic freedom works to everyone's benefit. As long as lenders and borrowers are free to strike their own terms, the collective results will be a success. However, as we will see later on, the market for loans can be distorted by outside forces. When it is, disaster usually ensues.

CHAPTER 3

THE MANY USES OF CREDIT

As we have just seen, Able decided to loan Baker and Charlie fish so that they could build nets. Business loans such as these are the best use of saved capital because they tend to expand production.

Of course, the act of lending money—or fish—to start a business is no guarantee that the venture will be successful. A borrower may not be able to fully execute on his initial plan.

That's what would have happened if Charlie and Baker failed to produce successful nets.

In other instances, a business may
fail because the idea never held
any promise to begin with.
Suppose instead of asking for
a loan to build a net, Baker
and Charlie asked Able for a
loan that would allow them to
perfect a technique for mass
fish hypnosis.

If the fish wouldn't fall for it, the loan would produce no
benefit for the borrowers—Charlie and Baker—or the
lender—Able.

The bottom line is that loans made to businesses that do
not succeed waste society's store of savings and diminish
productive capacity. As a result, the lender may then have
trouble getting back his principal, let alone the interest.

But the business plans that work make up for the ones that
don't!

It is important to understand that business loans are not the
only option for society's store of savings. There are other types
of loans that Able could have made—consumption loans and
emergency loans.

Consumption Loans

Suppose that rather than making a loan to Baker and Charlie
to build their own nets, Able had succumbed to their
demands for a loan so they could take a vacation.

✔ REALITY CHECK

Whenever an outside force, such as government, encourages or demands that savers make loans for reasons that may have nothing to do with the actual likelihood of repayment, higher degrees of loss are almost inevitable. Such distortions waste society's savings.

In their zeal to do something good, governments like to influence the way savings are lent out. They pass laws that make some types of loans more appealing than others. But government has no savings; only individuals do! If, as a result of government incentives, the loans go to individuals or businesses that fail to pay off (and they often do), then the loss falls to those individuals who have sacrificially under consumed to create savings!

In fact, Able would be much less inclined to lend in the first place if he were forced to make loans that he felt were excessively risky, such as in the case of fish hypnosis. As a result, he may decide not to work as hard, or not to sacrifice as much to save!

"Hey, Rocke-fisher," griped Baker. "Maybe you should take a break from fish counting and lend me and my pal Charlie a couple of fish so we can kick back a day or two. You're not the only one who deserves a life of leisure. And besides, we'll pay you back."

"Believe me, I know that fishing can get to be a drag," responded Able. "But remember, if I lend you one fish, I'll still want two fish in return to compensate me for the risk."

"No sweat, Kingfish," countered Charlie. "We'll be so well rested after our vacation, we'll be able to fish even harder and pay you back, with interest."

But how will Baker and Charlie be able to repay the vacation loan, with interest, if they do not expand their productive capacity? After taking a few days off, they will still only be able to catch one fish per day. To repay Able, they will need to cut their consumption to less than one fish per day in the future. Their living standards would have to drop to repay the loan!

Knowing this possible consequence, Able tried to be reasonable. "Look guys, why borrow now and go hungry to repay the loan, when you can just sacrifice now, go hungry for one day, build your own net, save up for the future, and then rest up whenever you want?"

"Listen," said Baker and Charlie. "Save the holier-than-thou bunk. Just give us the fish!"

32

Able should deny the loan. Not only would such a transaction put his savings at unnecessary risk, but it would mean that the capital would be unavailable for more productive loans. And while he will earn their scorn, he will actually prevent future hardship. In actuality, loans to consumers that do not fundamentally improve productive capacity are a burden to both the lenders and the borrowers.

Emergency Loans

As it turns out, Able's rejection of Baker and Charlie's "vacation" (consumption) loans was extremely fortunate. A week

later, both are struck by a freak outbreak of the Pokalani Pox, which prevents them from fishing for a week.

Now, when this emergency arises, Able is in a position to make a hardship consumer loan out of his accumulated savings so that Baker and Charlie can eat and live to work another day. Although he also understands that the risk of nonrepayment is high, he understands that the risk in not making the loan is higher. Unlike the consumption loan, Baker and Charlie can perish if the emergency loan is not made. If this were to happen, the island would lose productive capacity.

This emergency loan would not have been possible if Able had already given away his savings through unproductive consumer loans.

In fact, savings can mean the difference between the life and death of society.

✔ REALITY CHECK: CAN ABLE EXPAND CREDIT?

When confronted with the possibility of economic contraction, politicians and bankers frequently discuss the need to "expand credit" by increasing the amount of money available to be lent. But can this be done on command? In the case of our fishing friends, how can Able legitimately lend out more fish than he has saved? The island's total supply of credit is limited by its total supply of saved fish.

TAKEAWAY

U nfortunately, it is widely accepted that in order to spur activities that politicians and social theorists deem to be beneficial, government influences how savings are allocated. This has been accomplished by a litany of government loan guarantees and corporate and individual tax credits and penalties.

As a result of these influences, individuals and businesses may be more willing to apply for, and banks may be more willing to grant, certain types of loans. More of society's resources are then directed toward the favored activity, whether it be home building, college attendance, or solar panel manufacturing.

Central to these impulses is the notion that government planners have a better idea of what's good for society than savers themselves. But there is no evidence that this is true. In fact, history is littered with grandiose schemes hatched in government think tanks that have simply not delivered on their promise.

But more fundamentally, the imposition of a government layer in between savers and borrowers separates the cause and effect of lending, and leads to an inefficient allocation of savings.

Private lenders tend to be influenced only by the financial results of a loan, rather than the political symbolism of the underlying activity. Businesses that adhere to successful models and are run by owners with strong records of achievement tend to repay loans at higher rates. As a result, these types of business plans tend to attract willing lenders. Much like Darwin's idea that natural selection produces hardier species, this lending discipline tends to produce healthier companies and a stronger economy.

But this does not occur when financial performance becomes secondary. Loans made to individuals or enterprises that do not succeed in creating a needed innovation or expanding productive capacity tend to weaken the overall economy by wasting the supply of savings.

But as we will see later in the book, the creation of a constantly expanding money supply, and the government's seemingly limitless ability to take on debt, have hidden the fact that real credit is limited by a finite supply of savings.

People now assume that all that is needed for a functioning credit market is willing borrowers. But like any other resource, savings must be accumulated before it can be lent out.

CHAPTER
4
ECONOMIC EXPANSION

After a few weeks, Able, Baker, and Charlie had been raking in the fish with their newly built nets, and a two-fish-per-day catch had become the norm. After a threadbare one-fish- per-day diet, who could blame them? But having experienced the benefits that flow from self-sacrifice, they decided to save a good portion of that potential consumption. Every couple of days, they made do with just one fish apiece.

Released from the need to fish every waking moment, the islanders finally had the freedom to undertake other productive and enjoyable activities. Able was able to devote some time to designing and constructing more functional—and more flattering—palm-leaf clothing. Baker expanded his diet and culinary skills by gathering coconuts, and Charlie built the island's first hut.

Things were going well, but Baker was convinced they could be even better. He said, "If we can expand production with hand nets, why not kick it up a notch and go industrial?" He envisioned a larger and better piece of capital equipment.

He sketched out the plans for an elaborate fish-catching device that would revolutionize the island's economy. The gizmo involved a huge underwater trap with one-way doors that could catch fish continually day or night. That's right— fish check in, but they don't check out. If it worked, they would never have to fish again!

But, Baker soon realized that the he was unable to handle such a complex project by himself. He thought about the materials necessary, the netting, the framework, the construction. His savings, brawn, and ingenuity were simply not enough for such a colossal project.

With these thoughts in mind, Baker decided to propose a joint venture. The three could form a company, underconsume for a while, pool their savings, and dedicate an entire week to construction.

Having listened to Baker's plan, they began to discuss the potential risks. As with Able's first net, there was no guarantee that the project would work. Even if it did, the whole contraption could fall apart in its first exposure to rough seas. But this time it wasn't just one fish they were risking, but more than 20!

However, their demand for more fish overpowered their fear of losing their savings.

They moved forward.

After a supreme effort, the three succeeded in building the island's first mega fish catcher. The trap delivered as advertised and racked up an average of 20 fish per week, with no fuss and barely any muss. Outside of some minor repairs and maintenance, the trap was almost entirely automated. Soon they were swimming in fish.

With the savings that quickly piled up due to this latest advancement in productivity, the three soon built another mega fish catcher.

Fish became so abundant that they were able to dedicate all their time to other projects.

Charlie used his savings to build surfboards, resulting in a new ultracool leisure activity.

Able used his savings to establish a clothing company that would produce items not just for himself but for any islander who wanted to freshen up their image. In his spare time, he began working on his one-man stage play.

For his part, Baker used his free time to focus on the island's vexing transportation problems, and developed designs for the island's first canoe and cart.

✔ REALITY CHECK

Savings are not just a means to increase one's ability to spend. They are an essential buffer that shields economies from the unexpected.

Suppose a monsoon came through the island and wiped out both mega fish catchers? Although many economists today view natural disasters as stimulative to an economy, the truth is floods, fires, hurricanes, and earthquakes destroy wealth and diminish living standards. If the fish catchers were wiped out, the island's fish production would drop, and Able, Baker, and Charlie would have to underconsume again in order to generate savings to rebuild their capital.

But, remember, a pool of spare savings prevents disruption and allows for immediate reconstruction of damaged capital. That is why it is essential that Able, Baker, and Charlie continue to underconsume and save for a rainy day.

TAKEAWAY

In the past, the United States was known as a nation of savers. Throughout much of our history American citizens typically saved 10 percent or more of their incomes annually. This discipline not only helped build a huge supply of savings to finance our growing industrial activity, but it also helped families and communities endure unexpected hardships.

However, in recent years, economists have severely downgraded savings on the economic value chain. In fact, as far as many economists are concerned, savings are a drag. Keynesians view savings as detrimental to growth because the act removes money from circulation and decreases spending (which they assume is the crucial element in creating economic growth). Policy makers, influenced by these ideas, have made rules that reward spenders and penalize savers.

As a result, Americans have, for years, spent more than we have earned. In a contained economy, like an island, this would be impossible. But in our modern world, the flow of money across borders and the seemingly magical qualities of the printing press have temporarily blinded many Americans to the simple truth that we can't consume more than we produce, or borrow more than we save…at least not for very long.

When the economic headwinds began to pick up in earnest in 2008, politicians and economists reflexively looked for a means to get consumers to spend even more and save even less.

They have it backward. Spending for its own sake means nothing. What if you spent $1 million, but bought nothing but air? How would this benefit society? It would surely benefit the person who sold you the air. He would get the million dollars formerly belonging to you. Using our modern methods of economic accounting, such as the measurement of gross domestic product (GDP), such a transaction would certainly look like genuine activity. It would be counted as $1 million worth of growth.

But the act of buying air does not improve the economy as a whole. The air was always there. Something has to be produced to give the spending any value.

Spending is merely the yardstick that we use to measure production. Since everything that is produced will eventually be consumed, why does spending really matter? Even the stuff that no one really wants will be consumed if the price falls far enough. But nothing can be consumed until it is produced. It's production that adds the value.

Saving creates the capital that allows for the expansion of production. As a result, a dollar saved makes more of a positive economic impact than a dollar spent. Just don't try to explain this to an economist or a politician.

CHAPTER 5

PROSPERITY LOVES COMPANY

The same economic rules that operate in a simple economic society also apply to a more complicated one....

Able's initial willingness to create capital through his own personal sacrifice benefited the other islanders. As a result of his prudent lending program, the islanders built many hand nets, and then capitalized on the increased productivity to fund much more efficient fish-catching machines. In addition to allowing a better diet, more flattering attire, and easier transport, the increased productivity gave rise to leisure time and a burgeoning surfing scene.

Tales of this unprecedented luxury soon spread to other islands, where fishing was still done by hand and no one had time to surf. In search of a better life, immigrants soon arrived.

The greater productivity of the island meant that it could support a greater population, which in turn led to greater economic diversity. Some new immigrants went to work servicing the mega fish catchers, while others borrowed the extra fish to clear the land for farming—at last a balanced diet! Others took out loans to go into other trades.

The diversified island economy soon gave rise to hut builders, canoe builders, wagon builders, you name it.

Society had become so good at producing food and tools that some people didn't need to produce anything physical to survive. As a result, a service sector was born.

Looking to improve on the delectability of the raw fish, some islanders developed specialized systems of fish preparation, often involving spices and fire. The skills of these chefs became so highly prized that the more prosperous fishermen and hut builders would pay them fish in exchange for their delectable food and culinary skills.

Other service jobs developed soon after.

The allure and social benefits of surfing became so widely prized that Charlie's descendants founded a surfing school.

As the society grew and more trades and services were offered, a medium of exchange was needed so that the hut builder, chef, or surfing instructor could be paid.

Up till now, the island had functioned on a barter system, where one person traded one good or service for another. But this process was cumbersome and inefficient. A spear maker may want a chef, but a chef may not want a spear. Even if their desires did converge, how many cooked meals would a spear be worth, anyway?

To replace this system of haphazard deal making, the island needed something that could be traded for anything and that was accepted by everybody. In other words, they needed money.

Since everyone on this island ate fish, it was decided that fish would serve as money.

In short order, all wages and prices were quoted in terms of fish. And since subsistence was still imagined at one fish per day, one fish had a value to which everyone could relate. The island's price structure therefore was related to the real (or intrinsic) value of fish.

Efficiency and Deflation

An economy in which workers can specialize in a specific trade or service is always better than one where everyone does the same thing. Specialization increases production, which in turn raises living standards.

Let's say that it took the average islander five days to make a canoe. If it is assumed that every islander could catch two fish per day (with a net), then each person would have to forgo 10 fish of income in order to build a canoe. However, suppose one islander named Duffy was a little better at cutting, hauling, and chopping wood and could make a canoe in just four days.

Rather than fishing like everybody else, Duffy would be much better off if he just made canoes. As he would only have to defer eight fish in income to build a canoe, he could make a profit by charging nine fish for one of his canoes. He could raise his income through specialization.

Given these advantages, other islanders would be wise to buy one of Duffy's canoes for nine fish. (Left to themselves, they would have to give up 10 fish in income.) By paying only nine to a specialist, they could save one fish.

But suppose nine fish represented a fairly steep price…after all, who has that many fish just lying around? Perhaps at those prices only the wealthiest islanders could afford a new canoe. Those who didn't have that level of accrued savings would just have to keep swimming until they had saved enough to pull the trigger.

But let's imagine that after years of cutting and shaping his logs with rocks and sharp shells, Duffy used **his** accumulated savings to build specialized canoe-making tools. Like Able many generations before, he was underconsuming in order to generate a capital good (tools).

Because of his better equipment, let's also imagine that Duffy cut his building time down to two days. With this increased efficiency, he would now only have to charge four fish instead of eight fish per canoe to break even. If he lowered his price to six fish (from nine) he would be more profitable on each canoe he sold (two fish per canoe instead of one), and he would be able to crank out twice as many units.

This increased productivity benefited not only Duffy, but all the islanders. More could afford a canoe priced at just six fish, so his customer base increased.

As a result of this improved efficiency—made possible by savings, innovation, and investment—the price for canoes came down and the benefits of canoe ownership became available to a wider pool of buyers. What was once a luxury for the rich became common for everyone.

✔ REALITY CHECK

As echoed in the preceding tale, falling prices don't hurt Duffy. In fact, as prices for all things come down through similar productivity gains in other industries, the fish he earns will enable him to buy more things.

Innovation is a one-way process. Unless people forget what they already know, efficiency always compounds. As a result, prices tend to come down over time.

Steadily dropping prices also encourage savings as islanders begin to understand that their fish would likely buy more goods in the future than they do today. As crazy as it sounds, a fish saved is indeed a fish earned. This encourages savings, thereby swelling the amount of capital available for loans.

Employment

As the society became more complex, more and more islanders decide to work for other people by trading their labor for wages.

The value of labor is always multiplied by the use of capital. The better the capital, the more valuable the labor. For instance, you can dig a bigger hole with a bulldozer than with a shovel, even if you work just as hard with both. Thus, it's best to work with the best capital available.

In a free society all the residents decide for themselves whose capital to use to magnify the value of their labor. Putting aside those who metaphorically choose to fish without a net (perhaps for artistic reasons), each worker is free to:

- Underconsume to build a net.
- Take out a business loan to buy a net.
- Work for someone who already has a net.

As the first option requires underconsumption, and the second option involves risk, most workers choose the third option. If they do, they are paid wages.

For instance, Finnigan, a new arrival on the island, was a very strong man. His talents were wasted as a fisherman, so he decides to specialize in fish transport. Relying solely on his brawn, Finnigan was able to deliver 100 fish per day from the beach to people's huts. At a 2 percent freight charge, Finnigan could earn two fish per day working for himself.

However, having previously taken out a business loan to build a fish cart, Murray's Cart Company was stiff competition. Using his own cart, Murray could deliver 300 fish per day, even though he was not nearly as strong as Finnigan. Based on his high level of productivity, he charged only a 1 percent rate, thereby earning three fish per day. So because of his capital he was able to charge a lower rate and still earn more than Finnigan.

Without his own capital, Finnigan was in a pickle.

Assuming that the burlier guy could deliver 400 fish a day with a cart, Murray sensed an opportunity. As Finnigan could generate four fish per day in income with the cart (using the 1 percent delivery rate), Murray offered him three fish per day as an employee. Murray could keep the fourth fish as profit.

If Finnigan took the job, he would increase his productivity, lower his delivery rate, and earn more than he could by himself.

With the one-fish-per-day profit, Murray could stop delivering the fish himself, and focus on building more carts and expanding his business by hiring more delivery people. Meanwhile, proliferation of carts will bring down freight costs for all islanders.

Hopefully, at some point down the road, Finnigan could save up his income and build his own cart to compete against his former boss. In order to prevent this from happening, Murray would have to pay Finnigan more than he could have gotten on his own, and enough to discourage him from leaving the company.

But Murray's potential for profit is the sole motivation for all of this. He doesn't intend to help out Finnigan, but he does so inadvertently. The result is a better-paid worker and lower costs for all.

TAKEAWAY

There is no greater propaganda victory in economics today than the complete vilification of *deflation* (and the relative acceptance of *inflation*). As far as economists and politicians are concerned, deflation, which is defined as the overall decline of prices over time, is the economic equivalent of the bubonic plague. At the slightest whiff of deflation, governments will typically enact policies to push prices back up.

But what's wrong with falling prices? Habituated as we have become to steadily rising prices, it would shock just about everyone to know that prices in the United States fell steadily for almost 150 years...from the late 1700s all the way to 1913! But during that time we experienced some of the fastest economic growth in the history of the planet. This was made possible for the precise reasons described in this chapter: increased efficiency. When combined with a stable supply of money (as existed in the United States until the establishment of the Federal Reserve), efficiency will push prices down.

The vastly increased productivity of the industrial revolution made it possible for working-class people to afford all kinds of goods, like upholstered furniture, tailored clothing, plumbing, and wheeled transportation, that were previously available only to the rich. Deflation meant that $100 saved in 1850 could buy many more goods and services in 1880. Why is this not a good thing? While modern grandparents habitually point out how much cheaper stuff was when they were kids, their own grandparents likely told stories to them about how much more expensive things were in their youth.

Yet despite the obvious benefits of lower prices, we still fear deflation. We are told that if prices were to fall, people would stop buying, companies would stop spending, workers would lose their jobs, and we would all return to the economic dark ages.

But we all see time and time again how falling prices do not deter particular industries. In the early twentieth century, Henry Ford made a fortune, and his workers became the best paid in the industry, by steadily bringing down the price of cars. More recently the computer industry has made bundles of money despite the fact that its products constantly experience significant price deflation. Yet despite plunging prices the computer revolution continues unabated. As a result of this efficiency in design and manufacture, millions and millions of people each year spend less and less to experience the marvels of digitization.

Despite this, most people assume that deflation is okay if it's confined to just one industry. Why would that be?

Modern economists mistakenly assume that spending drives growth, and that when deflation is present, people tend to defer purchases (to allow prices to fall); and when they do spend, the diminished price makes less of an economic impact. This is absurd.

As we've said before, it's not the spending that means anything. It's the production that counts!

People do not need to be persuaded to spend. Given that human demand is essentially endless, if people don't want something there is likely a good reason. Either the product is no good or the consumer simply cannot afford to buy it. Either way, the act of deferring a purchase, or saving instead of spending, is made for rational reasons and tends to benefit the economy as a whole.

In fact, if consumers are not spending, the best way to spur demand is to allow prices to fall to more affordable levels. Sam Walton made billions with this simple concept.

Despite all the exculpatory evidence, deflation remains economic enemy number one. This is because inflation (the opposite of deflation), is every politician's best friend. More about this later.

CHAPTER
6

PUT IT IN THE VAULT

GOOD BANK
Sea D

As the islander's fish-savings increased, storage became an issue. People traditionally kept fish in their huts, but that proved too inefficient and even dangerous. Fish filchers became a big problem.

And while the islanders would have liked to use their excess savings to grow through loans and investments, most individual savers had neither the time nor the training to judge the merits of business propositions offered to them.

Sensing a solid business opportunity, an islander named Max Goodbank decided to launch a revolutionary service.

After guarding his own fish for years, Max knew there had to be a better way to store his savings. And after seeing so many of his neighbors get hoodwinked by slick fish borrowers, he also knew that most people needed help in deciding how their savings should be lent. With these thoughts in mind, he built a large, climate-controlled facility staffed by the toughest galoots on the island. The new "bank" would safely store the island's collective fish savings and consequently solve the theft problem. But this was just the beginning....

Being a true entrepreneur, Max knew that if all he did was charge a storage fee, his profit potential would be limited.

He understood the value of savings and he knew he could do a better job at lending than a typical islander. As a top-notch mathematician, Max was particularly good at evaluating business plans and structuring equitable loans.

With the fish earned from the loans of his neighbor's fish, he would pay interest to depositors and wages to his galoots. He would keep the leftover profit for himself.

The Goodbank Savings and Loan was born!

Just like Able and Duffy, Max initially sought to benefit his own pocketbook. But to do so, he helped solve the island's thorny issues of savings, credit, and theft.

Now, when the "Ables" of the island underconsume, they delegate their investment responsibility to Goodbank by depositing their fish savings in his bank.

Those requiring loans in order to finance capital projects, need only see Mr. Goodbank rather than anyone who seemed to be sitting on a tidy pile of fish.

For the scheme to work, Max had to keep a number of balls in the air at once. First, he had to keep his loan business profitable, which meant he had to carefully screen borrowers, scrupulously collect interest, and foreclose on collateral when loans failed. Second, he had to keep his depositors happy through regular interest payments. Last, he had to attract more borrowers to keep the cycle running. If he failed, he would be out of a job, and his investment would be wasted.

Naturally, with his ability to specialize in the tasks associated with efficient and profitable lending, Max became the island's foremost expert on fish economics. And whereas less specialized lenders tended to be influenced by factors such as personal history, family relationship, and emotion, with Goodbank, it all boiled down to dollars and cents, or rather fins and scales.

Interest Rates

With his personal well-being so intertwined with the success of the bank, Max was in the ideal position to determine the best interest rates to pay depositors and to charge borrowers.

On the lending side, he offered the lowest interest rate to the most secure borrowers (those with the highest ability to repay the loans). For dicier borrowers he charged a higher rate to compensate for the added risk.

These loan rates then determined how much interest the bank could pay depositors, who received payments on a similarly sliding scale. Longer-held deposits lowered the bank's risk of a fish shortage. Accordingly, higher interest payments were offered to those willing to leave their fish on

deposit for a while. People who could not commit to a longer time frame got lower rates.

Although Goodbank administered the rates, the entire interest rate system itself fluctuated according to market conditions that were largely beyond Goodbank's control.

Sometimes big gains in productivity made the island's savings swell. When the vault was filled to the rafters with fish, the bank would be willing to drop the rates charged on loans. That was because the losses would be easier to bear in relative terms, and the healthy economy that produced the savings in the first place would provide a fertile environment for new businesses.

With little need to attract new savings, and with lower rates charged to borrowers, such an environment would also lead to lower payments to depositors, which would discourage savings.

When savings dipped (which is dangerous for an economy), opposite forces would come into play that would tend to encourage savings, thereby replenishing bank coffers.

When the fish were few, Goodbank had to be extra careful with loans. With thin reserves, loan defaults could be critical. In order to compensate for the increased relative risk, Max charged higher rates to borrowers, and offered higher rates to depositors in order to encourage more savings.

Higher interest rates would discourage borrowing and slow business growth. But the higher rates would also encourage savings. Eventually coffers would build up again and rates would then start to drop.

In addition, a lower savings rate indicated a preference for more immediate consumption. As a result, long-term capital investments designed to provide goods for future consumption would be discouraged.

This cyclical interest rate mechanism—firmly regulated by the desire to maximize the returns on the bank's deposits, the fear of losing capital on risky ventures, and individual time preferences for consumption—produced a rate of interest that would stabilize the market.

Most importantly, the safety and convenience of the bank encouraged people to save. Deferring consumption to a later date provided financing for capital projects that would increase future production and raise living standards.

Under Mr. Goodbank's wise and conservative care, the island's savings and commerce continue to grow.

High-Risk Investment

Given his need to continually pay interest to his depositors, Mr. Goodbank tended to shy away from loans that had a high probability of default. He refused to risk the islanders' savings on vacation loans, consumption loans, or any other "fish in the dish" ideas that promised the moon but could offer no realistic assumptions about potential success.

But some savers wanted to take greater risks for greater rewards. Occasionally potential breakthrough projects came along that were very enticing, but ultimately just too risky for the bank to fund.

Sling-Flight Airways pitched an idea that could revolutionize interisland travel.

But Goodbank, true to form, didn't bite.

But that didn't mean that the backers of Sling-Flight were out of options.

A new investment pool had arrived on the scene, run by the flamboyant fish tycoon Manny Fund. Manny took in fish from savers who were not content with the modest returns paid by Goodbank. With these fish he rolled the dice on high-profile projects.

Some of the projects he funded worked out, like the Paradise Beverage Company.

And others did not, like the Blubmarine Underwater Tour Company.

So, while Goodbank continued to finance capital growth through conservative forms of investment, Manny Fund became the choice for the risk takers.

TAKEAWAY

In addition to distorting the credit market by passing laws that favor certain types of loans and certain types of borrowers, government also influences the flow of credit in a more fundamental manner: through its control of interest rates. For almost 100 years, the Federal Reserve (in theory a private bank, but in practice an extension of the Treasury Department), has set the base level for interest rates upon which the entire rate structure rests.

By setting its "federal funds" rate higher or lower, the Fed (as the bank is known) does not dictate the particular rate any bank offers for every loan, but it does move the entire market up or down. Banks will always charge a higher rate to the public than they pay the Fed to borrow money. So when the Fed raises or lowers its rates, businesses and individuals will pay more, or less, to borrow.

The Fed was given this authority in order to keep the economy running smoothly in good times and bad. The theory goes that the collective wisdom of Fed economists could help keep the economy on track by determining the optimal interest rate for any particular moment in time.

For instance, the Fed could boost a struggling economy by lowering interest rates to the point where businesses and consumers would be more inclined to borrow. In very good times, when overconfidence often leads to foolishness, the Fed is supposed to do the opposite and raise rates so that people will think twice about taking out loans.

This system has two massive flaws.

First, it assumes that a small group of people at the Fed can make better decisions than millions of people making independent decisions (also known as "the marketplace") about the proper level of interest rates. But, the Fed has "no skin in the game," as the saying goes. It does not generate the savings and will not suffer if loans go bad. The people saved the money and the bank's profits depend on its wise stewardship. Without this connection, lending is inherently inefficient.

Second, the Fed's decisions are always determined by political, rather than economic, considerations. As low rates tend to make the economy appear better on the surface, push down the cost of servicing mortgages and other loans, and help financial firms make money, there are a great many people who want lower rates. Presidents seeking reelection will always bang the drum for lower rates, and they will pressure the Fed to help out. On their part, Fed policy makers naturally want to be seen as the good guys who help the economy, not the tight-fisted Scrooges who push it into recession.

The members of society who would favor high rates, most notably the savers, have no well-organized interest group. Their voices are never heard. As a result, there is a consistent bias toward holding rates too low, rather than too high. Remember, low rates encourage borrowing and discourage saving. Not surprisingly, the United States has been transformed from a nation of savers to a nation of borrowers.

In addition, rates that are too low relative to the supply of savings send false signals to borrowers about the health of the economy and the viability of investments. Since consumption has not really been deferred to the future (which would be the case had interest rates fallen due to market forces), capital investments intended to satisfy future consumption will be much less likely to succeed. The result is phony booms followed by spectacular busts, such as those just experienced in stocks and real estate.

CHAPTER 7

INFRASTRUCTURE AND TRADE

Traditionally islanders drew their drinking water from the mountain streams and carried it to their huts in whatever vessel they could fashion.

As a result, most people didn't live or work very far from the water supply. Poor access to water also made farming very difficult. These realities limited the island's overall productivity.

One year, a terrible drought descended and dried up many of the mountain streams. The hardship just about wiped everybody out.

The islanders searched for a solution that could prevent such a calamity in the future.

The fertile mind of Able Fisher V (Able's great-great-great-grandson) tackled the problem. He noticed that rain runoff collected in ponds. Taking his cue from nature, he devised a runoff and reservoir system where rainwater could be collected and stored for future use. But this would be a big project, furnishing the entire island with water.

As Able V conceived it, the Water Works project would require working capital of 182,500 fish…enough to support a crew of 250 men for two years while they labored. He went to Manny Fund for a loan. Manny loved the idea but he just didn't have enough fish. Fearing the worst, Able then tried the bank.

To his surprise, Maxine Goodbank (another descendant) had a receptive ear! Although the price was indeed high, when weighed against the potential rewards, the risk seemed justified. If it worked, the project would pay for itself and ensure a better future for every islander!

But no matter how much she liked the idea, Goodbank would not have been able to finance the project if the island had not saved enough to pay for it. There simply would not have been spare fish to feed 250 non-fishing workers for two years.

But upon completion, the Water Works delivered as advertised and allowed the borrowers to pay back their loan plus interest.

Islanders were happy to pay yearly fish fees for the running water. From these payments, Water Works employed more than 100 workers year-round to tend the system's intricate bamboo pipe system.

The splashing success of the Water Works project flowed through the island's economy. Pipelines, available for a reasonable charge, brought water great distances, and allowed previously infertile land to produce crops.

The steady flow of water could be harnessed to operate machines, giving birth to new industries.

Relieved of the task of hauling water by hand, everybody now had more time available for the production of consumer goods and services and for the development of new capital projects. The increased productivity allowed society to catch even more fish, and living standards rose as a result.

Trade

As the island economy expanded, its ability to export production abroad increased as well. Soon giant cargo canoes were sailing over the open ocean, fully loaded with fish, carts, surfboards, spears, and canoes. In exchange for these products, which had gained an ocean wide reputation for quality and affordability, the cargo canoes returned with fresh fish and other trade goods previously unknown on the island.

As the island's explorers came into contact with other islands, trade developed that further stimulated growth. When allowed to flourish unhindered, free trade benefits everyone.

Some islands (or cities, countries, or even people for that matter) often have a relative abundance of something that others don't. Each person, country, or island will naturally use its own particular advantages to get the most reward for what it has.

For instance, the nearby island of Bongobia had a great quantity of—you guessed it—bongos. The natives had perfected the craft of bongo-making and their island was overgrown with the best trees for making bongos. As a result, there were so many bongos on the island that each individual drum was not worth much. As a domestic trade good, a pair of bongos didn't go too far.

One hundred miles from Bongobia, the island of Dervishia was populated by natives who were smitten with bongos. Unfortunately, their environment lacked the right kind of trees to make them. As a result, on Dervishia bongos were a scarce and valuable trade good. What the Devirshes did have was an abundance of coconut tanning oil. But the dark-skinned Dervishes had no need for UV protection, so tanning oil was nearly worthless to them.

But as fate would have it, the fair-skinned Bongobians suffered from chronic sunburn due to the island's unrelentingly sunny weather.

When the two islands finally made contact with one another, they instantly developed a robust trade in bongos and tanning oil. Each island used its competitive advantage to send the other island products that were more valuable overseas than they were at home. In this symbiotic arrangement, both islands benefited. Living standards rose...and well-toned drumming was achieved by all.

Trade on a national level is no different than labor specialization on a personal level. Each individual, or country, trades what it has in abundance, or what it does best, for the things that it doesn't have or can't easily make.

✔ REALITY CHECK: BIG vs. LITTLE ECONOMICS

Now that the island community is so much bigger than it was when there were just three guys fishing by hand, to some it may appear that the economics have changed...but have they?

Just as the principles of mathematics don't change with the size of the problem, basic economic principles do not change with the size of the economy. They're just harder to see because of the many layers that exist between savers and borrowers. But the direct relationship among self-sacrifice, savings, credit, investment, economic incentive, and social and economic progress are always the same.

TAKEAWAY

Infrastructure spending can make a huge impact on an economy. But such spending is helpful only if the benefits exceed the costs. If not, the projects waste resources and hinder growth.

Currently, many politicians and economists erroneously view infrastructure spending not as a near-term cost that may lead to long-term gain, but as an immediate means to create jobs and boost the economy. This view can lead to costly misallocations of resources and the unseen destruction of jobs in other areas.

Over the past half century the United States has vastly underinvested in infrastructure. The cost of undoing this neglect is a burden on the current economy. The payoff comes in the future, and only if the work is successful.

In our story, the 182,500 fish borrowed to build the Water Works were no longer available to fund other job-creating investments. That's a big chance to take. Had those fish instead been spent on a worthless infrastructure project, such as Alaska's famed "Bridge to Nowhere," the island's savings would have been squandered and 250 islanders would have wasted two years' labor.

For much of the early history of the United States, projects like the Water Works were often private sector initiatives. But given the inherent unpredictability about the success of these projects, in our age of nearly universal government control it seems inconceivable that such an undertaking could be funded, built, and operated equitably by profit-driven private companies. But in those days they were.

For example, the New York City subways were largely built by private companies and were operated outside of city control for almost four decades. Despite the staggering construction costs, the railroads were able to operate at a profit. What's more, the fare never went up in 40 years.

These days, it's very easy to convince voters that large public amenities—like sewers, highways, canals, and bridges that are meant to benefit everyone—need to be run by the government. Politicians have successfully argued that private companies, which are motivated solely by profit, would exploit the public at the earliest opportunity.

The evidence supporting these claims is largely emotional. What is far more certain is that the government's monopoly control of public projects and services almost always leads to inefficiency, corruption, graft, and decay.

When a government project experiences cost overruns or poor service, free market discipline does not come to the rescue. The government simply raises taxes to fill the gap. In so doing, it wastes societal resources, and living standards drop.

Trade suffers from similar misconceptions. In their quest to protect American jobs from overseas competition, the opponents of free trade ignore the benefits of imports and the hidden costs to consumers that result from restricted choice.

For instance, if a foreign manufacturer can deliver T-shirts to the United States that sell for less than domestically produced alternatives, then Americans can spend less on T-shirts.

The money saved would be available to be spent on other things....skateboards perhaps. This would benefit the skateboard companies that may still be located in the United States and that can deliver the most valuable product in their category.

But what about the workers of the domestic T-shirt manufacturers who lose their jobs? If their employers cannot find ways to compete more effectively in the T-shirt business, it is true that the workers will have to find other work. But it is not the aim of an economy to provide jobs. The goal is simply to maximize productivity.

Society as a whole is not helped by perpetuating inefficient use of labor and capital. If the United States no longer has a competitive advantage in T-shirts, it must find something else in which it does.

If trade barriers were erected to protect those jobs, the cost of T-shirts would stay high. People would have less money to spend on skateboards (for instance), and those manufacturers would suffer. And so while it's easy to put your finger on the job that is saved, it's impossible to see the job that was not created.

It makes no sense to waste our labor making things that can be produced more efficiently abroad. If we focus on the things that we can make more efficiently than anyone else, then we can trade those products for the things that others produce better. In the end we'll have more stuff.

Of course, the problem is that because of our artificially high currency, high taxes, and restrictive wage and labor laws, we just are not competitive in enough product categories. That has to change.

CHAPTER
8

A REPUBLIC IS BORN

In the beginning, the island had no government... compensation at least for the limited diet. Able, Baker and Charlie were old friends and worked out disputes amicably. But as simple societies grow more complex, there inevitably arises the need for some central authority.

With more people on the island, misunderstandings multiplied. When words failed to settle the matter, spears were often employed to bring about a resolution.

With no organized mutual defense apparatus, occasionally gangs of fish filchers would go on a rampage and make life miserable for the islanders.

Every now and then the island would be invaded by the Bongobians, who in addition to being great drummers were also fierce plunderers. When the Bongobians got their mojos working, no saved fish were safe.

It was evident that the islanders needed to band together for mutual protection and security. They needed some leadership. But handing out power is always a risky business. Once given, power is almost always abused.

After experimenting with a variety of vainglorious chieftains and other losers, the islanders decided to put together a government that would be accountable to the people and would be limited in its ability to take away the freedoms that had brought the island its prosperity in the first place. It was decided that the islanders would elect 12 senators, including a senator-in-chief with executive authority.

To protect the island from hostile invasion, the senate would create and oversee a navy of spear-packing war canoes.

To promote social stability, and to protect every islander's rights to life, liberty, and property, the senate would establish a system of courts to settle disputes, and a police squad to enforce the decrees of the judges.

And to promote commerce, the senate would build and maintain a series of lighthouses to protect sea traffic from the island's treacherous cliffs.

In order to finance this modest apparatus, the islanders agreed to pay a yearly fish tax. All the fish sent in to the government would go into a special government account at the bank. The senate would draw on these funds to meet its expenditures.

But as the island was populated by fiercely independent citizens, many were wary of investing too much power in too few hands.

In order to ensure that the senators did not play fast and
loose with the island's fish taxes, a constitution was drafted
that clearly authorized certain powers to the senate.
Powers not mentioned were reserved to the people alone.
Just in case there was any confusion as to what the senate
could and could not do, a supreme judge was put in place
to enforce the constitution and maintain a check on the
political ambitions of senators.

When the constitution was voted on and passed, the island
nation was dubbed the Republic of Usonia.

The new government wisely decided to not spend all the
fish it raised in taxes. The reserves could come in handy in
case an unexpected monsoon temporarily sapped the island's
ability to fish or if the Bongobians launched a new and more
elaborate raid.

And although the government did
keep a number of people on its
payroll—lighthouse keepers,
constables, judges, and navy
paddlers—everyone understood that
those jobs could exist only because
the government taxed society's producers. If producers didn't
send in fish, the government employees couldn't eat.

✔ REALITY CHECK

Because the islanders understood that government
spending was really the same as taxpayer spending, they
believed that it should be the taxpayers who decided how
the money was spent. As a result, voting was restricted to
those who paid tax.

It was also understood that taxes reduced the available pool
of savings on the island and limited the supply of investment
capital. But most island residents agreed that the commercial
benefits that flowed from increased island security, fewer
canoe wrecks, and a court system that enforced contracts
and disputes, more than compensated for the lost savings.

So far, so good. But there's always something...

TAKEAWAY

I t's a shame how few modern Americans really
understand how our country was founded on a radical
experiment in strictly limited government. Steeped in the
transformative philosophies of freedom, reason, and science
that flourished in the seventeenth and eighteenth centuries,
the Founding Fathers sought to create a completely new
relationship between people and government, whereby
sovereignty rested with the individual, whose rights where
inviolable.

In the early days after the War of Independence, in
exchange for the establishment of a national government,
which many Americans did not want, the U.S. Constitution
was conceived as a masterfully designed cage that would
prevent the "beast" of government from running amok. The
Constitution not only protected people from government,
but it also protected minorities from the tyrannies of
majorities.

The Constitution deliberately sought to segment powers
in the different branches of the federal government to
decentralize authority into the many states, and most
importantly to prevent the federal government from taking
any power it decided to take.

The result was a nation where individuals could be secure
in their personal liberty and possessions, and who were not
prevented from disposing of their assets in any way they saw
fit. The fact that these rights, unfortunately, did not apply
to all inhabitants of the new country, does not diminish

the audacity of the idea, which had never previously been codified in any other country.

Over time, that clarity of vision has been blurred. In times of crisis enough people become convinced that government needs more power and that people can get by with fewer liberties. In our current economic crisis, this trend has unfortunately gathered a great deal of steam.

In our desire to make the pain of economic contraction go away, we have forgotten that freedom involves risk. If government is obligated to cure all hardships, then no one is really free in the first place. Take away the freedom to fail and you have obliterated the freedom to succeed.

CHAPTER
9

GOVERNMENT GETS CREATIVE

ONE FISH

For many generations the island government functioned as planned. A series of wise and restrained rulers came and went, maintaining a strict focus on encouraging business expansion and personal savings. Taxes were comparatively easy to bear and regulation of industry remained light. As production expanded, businesses profited, prices steadily fell, and purchasing power rose. After a few generations, almost every family owned a canoe. Some families even had two or three.

Since it took only a few dedicated fishermen to provide for the island's entire nutritional needs, labor and capital were freed up for other purposes. New industries and services were developed that had been completely unknown in the days of hand fishing. Hut furnishings, witch doctoring, and drum making companies sprouted and flourished. Things got so prosperous that a theater troupe opened on the island's west coast. The premiere production of *The Fishman Cometh* opened to rave reviews.

Along the way, some senators made the emotional case that the Constitution's original linkage between tax payment and voting eligibility was fundamentally undemocratic. Out of a spirit of progressivism, this restriction was removed, bringing to the polls a great many voters who were far less interested in government budgetary prudence.

As the government payroll grew along with the economy, the job of senator inevitably gained in status and appeal. Originally a position for just the most revered and accomplished of the island's elders, the Senate now began to attract ambitious go-getters.

One of the more innovative of the senatorial hopefuls was Franky Deep, who noticed a strain in human behavior that provided him with a path to power.

He observed that people loved getting stuff for free. Similarly, they hated paying taxes. So, he devised a plan: if he could find a way to make it look like he was giving something to the islanders for free, then he could gain their unconditional support. Unfortunately, all the government had was what it raised in taxes. The Senate didn't catch any fish. They could only give by taking. How could they give more away more than they took?

After a particularly bad monsoon, Franky sensed an opportunity (politicians never let a crisis go to waste).

He preached, "My fellow islanders, the storm we have just been though has wrought untold hardship on our people. Many of our citizens are now hutless and fishless.

We cannot stand idly by and do nothing. If elected, I will institute a government reconstruction program for our neediest citizens to

repair the damage. But he assured the citizens that the cost of the construction would be paid for by the economic activity the spending generated.

His opponent, Grouper Cleveland, offered nothing, except wise stewardship of the island's savings and a promise not to interfere with the liberties of the citizenry.

Not surprisingly, Franky Deep sailed into office as Senator in Chief.

His election victory did not change the fact that there were not enough fish reserves to finance the spending plans he envisioned. To cover the gap, Franky came up with another plan. The government would issue paper money called Fish Reserve Notes, which would be redeemable for actual government fish stored at the Goodbank. Citizens could get their fish immediately or use the notes to trade for other goods and services just as they would have done with real fish.

Disgusted, the island's chief judge weighed in, and pointed out that the Constitution gave the Senate no authority to take money from one citizen for the sole benefit of another, nor did it have the authority to issue paper notes for fish.

Franky solved that problem by nominating one of his political buddies to sit as judge. The more cooperative jurist declared the Constitution to be a "living document" whose precepts could be actively interpreted by new generations confronting issues unforeseen by the founding fishers.

At first, the citizens were a little uncomfortable with the new Fish Reserve Notes. They were used to paying for things with actual fish. But after a while the new paper notes caught on. Most had to admit that they were easier to carry and the odor was a distinct improvement.

Meanwhile, Franky's advisors scoured the island looking for worthy projects to fund (maintaining unvarnished objectivity, of course). When they found a project that  would be guaranteed to have enough support from potential voters, they handed out the new notes to make it happen.

The new bank director, Max Goodbank VII, was not crazy about the new fish notes. He thought the ease in which the notes could be printed would create dangerous incentives for the senators. Yet, he could sleep soundly at night provided that the government maintained enough actual government fish in the bank to redeem all the notes.

Not surprisingly, his confidence didn't last long.

Soon, Franky and his agents had handed out far more Fish Reserve Notes than the government's account had fish to redeem. When Max Goodbank noticed the dwindling reserves, he headed to the Senate to sound the alarm.

"Franky, stop the presses!" shouted Max. "I have only nine fish available for every 10 notes that you guys have handed out. If the savers figure out that there really aren't enough fish to cover their deposits, there will be a run on the bank and I'll be out of fish. You have to stop issuing Fish Reserve Notes and raise taxes. We've got to replace our reserves."

Franky and his top advisors, Hughey Humpback and Tad Anemone, burst out laughing. "Raise taxes and cut spending...that's a good one! You'd be a real force on the campaign trail! Got any other bright ideas?"

Goodbank explained, "Sorry, guys, but there really is no choice. Once the savers on the island realize that there is really no safety in bank deposits, they'll stop saving! They'll keep their fish at home like they used to. There will be no pool of capital available to maintain the equipment we now rely on, much less to fund new projects! Our whole economy could collapse!"

"Listen, worrywart," said Franky. "We thought of that, and we have a plan. Why should the savers have to know that their savings are shrinking and not growing?"

Franky explained, "My economic advisors have degrees from our new University, where they mingled with some of the island's top scientists. It's amazing the things that some of these guys come up with. And they have really hit the jackpot. It's time that we let you in on a little secret. Bring in the technicians."

At that a number of lab-coated scientists walked in with three regular-looking fish. "Look!" said one. "We've been scouring the beaches and garbage dumps collecting discarded fish skins and skeletons…especially the ones with head and tail intact. Just watch the magic."

Then in a blur of cutting, splicing, gluing, and sewing, the technicians took the fish and began construction of a new fish around the discarded fish parts. They sculpted, molded, glued, and sealed. Using this process they were able to produce four passable fish out of the three. What was once garbage now looked like a genuine fish!

"The secret is in the glue," said Franky. "This new sealant never comes undone. The fish will hold together indefinitely, and the dupes…I mean citizens…will be none the wiser. We'll call these new fish 'official fish' and we'll use them to pay back the depositors. Let our boys into your vault for few days and your fish crunch problems will be solved!"

Goodbank was stunned. He had to admit that the trickery was impressive. The corners of his mouth crept up in a smile. He was tired of having to say "no" all the time. It was no fun. Nobody liked him…they called him a tightwad behind his back.

"Maybe this is the way out," he thought. "Maybe this is a ticket to popularity. First I get the fish…then I get the power…then I get the women!"

But then his good sense rushed back. "These people aren't magicians," he thought. "Fish don't grow on trees! All the senators can do is create fake fish by diminishing the value of the island's savings!" He tried to reason with them.

"Come on, the depositors will get wise. Look, your 'official fish' looks skimpy next to a genuine fish! After all, people have been eating fish a long time around here. Everyone knows the value of a fish. They may not be that easy to fool."

Answering in his most diplomatic voice, Franky tried to calm Goodbank's fears. "We thought of that. So for a start, 'official fish' won't need to be too much smaller. We'll make 10 official ones out of every nine real ones, so they'll be only 10% smaller. In addition—and this is the genius part—we'll pass a law to prevent islanders from comparing them to real fish!"

Tad Anemone chimed in, "Yes, that's right. We'll say our scientists have discovered a new disease among unprocessed fish, and we'll require everyone to turn in their genuine fish for officially decontaminated fish as soon as they are caught!"

The senators and technicians described how the decontamination process would explain why "official fish" were not quite as filling.

To keep people from seeing real fish themselves, and to supposedly increase fish production, the senators also decided to establish a Fishing Department, which would have sole responsibility for catching fish.

Goodbank could take no more of this. "This can't work! If people stop fishing for themselves and rely on the government instead, our total catch will diminish. Eventually we will run out of savings."

"How can you be so sure?" countered Franky. "Our Fishing Department will be the wave of the future. We'll put in only our most trusted friends as managers, and we'll give special prizes to the workers who show the greatest civic spirit. And besides, we only need to keep it going through the next election. After that we'll think up a more long-term plan…. I promise we will."

"In the meantime," said Hughey Humpback, "this new fish expansion procedure will give you enough fish to cover all of your outstanding obligations and pay all the interest on your deposits. We will even have fish left over to spend in ways that will finally do some good for our people!"

Goodbank thought about it some more. "It can't work. The people will get wise. They will worry about their savings and withdraw their deposits."

"We've got that covered," explained Franky. "We will declare that all deposits will be guaranteed by a new government agency called the Fish Deposit Insurance Corporation (FDIC for short). Once people know that the senate stands behind their deposits, who's going to withdraw their fish? With insurance in place, depositors will think that we are protecting their savings even while we loot its value."

"So, Max," said Franky, leaning in close and giving him a squeeze around the shoulders. "You'll go along, won't you?"

Goodbank was tempted to throw his lot in with the reformers, but he found his spine. While the 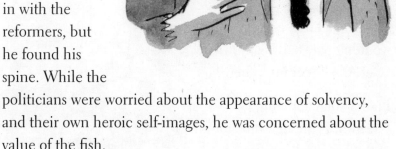 politicians were worried about the appearance of solvency, and their own heroic self-images, he was concerned about the value of the fish.

"Absolutely NOT!" he thundered. "It's fraud...deception! If there's one trait you senators have in common, it's dishonesty! I'll close the bank and tell the people to save their fish at home before I go along with this."

During this tirade the senators rolled their eyes and shrugged their shoulders, and eventually they could take no more. Franky summoned the Senate guards. He whispered a few words to the chief guard, and Goodbank was hauled away kicking and screaming…his parting words falling on deaf ears.

"It's too bad that chump wouldn't play ball," said Franky. "Get Ally Greenfin in here!"

Franky then appointed Greenfin as the new director of the bank with strict instructions to implement the fish expansion plan at full tilt. Furthermore, the Goodbank Savings and Loans would now be called the Fish Reserve Bank.

The next morning the body of Max Goodbank VII, the island's trusted banker, was found tangled in the coral reef. The death was attributed to natural causes. Eulogies, bathed in crocodile tears, echoed from the highest halls on the island. Senator Franky ordered a lavish funeral.

With Ally Greenfin now chairman of the Fish Reserve Bank, the scheme worked to perfection. The transition from genuine fish to "official fish" was made....

TAKEAWAY

As discussed earlier, the United States experienced sustained deflation for most of its history. Then in 1913, the Federal Reserve was established. The notes it issued, which promised to pay the bearer gold on demand, replaced the private bank notes then in circulation, which offered similar guarantees. But as soon as the Fed came on the scene, prices started rising steadily.

The Fed, as the Federal Reserve is known, was originally given the mission of establishing an "elastic money supply." The idea would be that the Fed could expand or contract the amount of money in circulation to correspond with economic activity. It was thought that such movements could hold prices steady through good times and bad.

Even if such a mission were a good idea to begin with, it's easy to see that the Fed has utterly failed in accomplishing it.

Over the past 100 years, the dollar has lost more than 95 percent of its value. So much for price stability! The truth is that the Fed now exists for the sole purpose of providing the inflation necessary to allow the government to spend more than it collects in taxes.

During the Depression, President Roosevelt decided to devalue the dollar against gold. In order to pull this off, the government had to control the entire gold market, and for a time the government made it illegal to own gold coins. Later on the ability to redeem the notes for gold was restricted to just banks, then to just foreign banks, and then finally to no one.

We are left with a currency that has no real value and can be expanded at will. This has prevented the government from ever having to make hard choices about spending and taxes, and has set us on a path that will eventually destroy the remaining value of the dollar.

CHAPTER 10

SHRINKING FISH

The senators could not believe their good fortune. They could now make campaign promises and spend at will! There was no reason to balance the budget or raise taxes to pay for the spending.

So every year the government issued more Fish Reserve Notes than the bank had savings to redeem. When the deposits got low, the fish technicians worked their magic. The mix proved to be intoxicating. And despite their gnawing urge to contain the situation, and to get back to a sustainable path, the senators just couldn't help themselves.

Some of the projects funded by government provided some benefit to all. The island navy got bigger canoes, which kept the Bongobians at bay; and a new system of cart paths made transportation easier. However, the benefits provided by the controversial Clean Rocks Jobs Program were much harder to quantify. But whether shiny rocks were something the island actually needed did not diminish the program's popularity to those who got the jobs.

Meanwhile the new government Fishing Department got up and running. By offering generous benefits and salaries, the department easily hired workers. Those who got the jobs loved the steady work, and happily voted for their senatorial patrons.

But beneath the surface, there were real problems brewing.

With no personal incentives to take risks and make profits, the Fishing Department failed to become a model of efficiency.

The rate of increase of actual fish production did not rise as fast as the supply of Fish Reserve Notes that the Senate put into circulation.

Soon so many Fish Reserve Notes had been issued that the technicians had to increase the conversion rate. Ten to nine gave way to five to four. This meant that official fish were now 20 percent smaller than real fish.

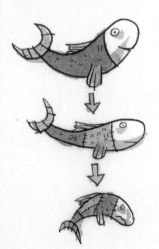

When that proved insufficient, the conversion dropped to three to two, and eventually two to one.

As official fish became smaller and smaller, it soon became apparent that the islanders could no longer survive on just one fish per day. Most now ate two per day, at minimum.

Given that fish were used as money on the island, prices for everything had to go up to keep pace with the diminished nutritional value of fish. The nagging problem of "fishflation" was born. So while efficiency had traditionally driven prices down, now government-created fishflation forced them in the opposite direction.

Strangely, no one could agree on why prices were going up. Ally Greenfin offered a needed theory. "Fishflation," he said, "is caused by a phenomenon known as the 'cost-price-fish push.'" He argued that high employment (thanks in part to government jobs) combined with a strong economy creates greater demand for fish and forces up prices.

As proof of their prosperity Greenfin noted that most islanders were now eating twice as many fish as their parents.

Greenfin warned that without the stimulus that is provided
by a steady dose of fishflation, people would lose their
appetites, and stop demanding fish, and the island economy
would contract. He further theorized that a fishflation level
of only one-half of a fish belly per year would be optimal.
Fishflation, he argued, was essential to an expanding
economy!

"Nice figuring, Ally. You could talk a shark out of a fish
barrel," said Franky. But nobody thought of pointing a finger
at government, the real cause of fishflation!

With a blank check to do whatever it wanted, the government
continued to curry favor with citizens by issuing more and
more Fish Reserve Notes. As it did, the official fish continued
to shrink in size and the fish became less and less valuable.
Wages and prices, therefore, had to go up. Although in some
years the fishflation was barely noticeable because of offsetting

productivity gains, two things were certain: the fish never got bigger, and prices rarely went down!

When fishflation became rapid, islanders finally noticed that the fish they withdrew from the bank were smaller than the fish they deposited. So, despite the enticement of interest paid on their savings, they began to save less while many discontinued saving completely. Instead, fish had to be spent quickly to avoid losses due to rapidly increasing prices.

The real burden of this rapid fishflation fell on retirees. Those who had deposited fish in the bank during their working years found that they had to eat two or three fish per day just to survive. The savings that they had hoped would last for 20 years, were gone in just four or five.

Since fishflation discouraged saving, bank deposits dwindled. As a result, there were less fish available to fund promising projects or prop up sagging businesses. In response, businesses cut back and workers were laid off. Desperate to offset the effects of fishflation, many more islanders decided to risk thier savings with Manny Fund, whose promise of oversized returns gave investors the best hope of overcoming these losses.

When unemployment reached a crisis level, people demanded that the government do something.

In response, the Senate set strict limits on how much companies could pay workers, under what circumstances the workers could be hired and fired, and how much the businesses could charge for their products. The resulting constraints made it more difficult to do business, and limited the ability of businesses to grow.

As time passed, a new senator, Lindy B., saw another electoral opportunity…this time to make a Great Society! Lindy promised that if elected not only would he furnish the canoe navy with bigger spears, but he would also help the sagging economy by providing emergency unemployment fish notes to all laid-off workers.

His opponent, Buddy Goldfish, offered nothing but careful stewardship of the island's savings and boring protection for the islanders' economic liberties. More importantly, Buddy argued that the island could not afford such an extravagant "spears and fish" policy.

Not surprisingly, Lindy won in a landslide.

And so the process continued. Fish Reserve Notes were produced in ever greater numbers while the fishing fleet returned with fewer and fewer actual fish.

As official fish shrank to just one-tenth of their former size, even Ally Greenfin knew that he could not stretch the fish skin any further. When there were just bones left in the vault, he ran over to the Senate and called an emergency meeting.

TAKEAWAY

One of the reasons that economists have been so successful in obscuring the source of inflation is that they have short-circuited the very definition of the word. Nearly everyone believes that rising prices means inflation. So if prices aren't rising, there must be no inflation.

But rising prices are merely the results of inflation! The inflation is the expansion of the money supply.

Any dictionary printed before 1990 defines inflation purely as an expansion of the money supply. Newer editions have hedged their bets. But if you understand the true definition, you know that it is possible that prices can stay flat, or even fall, while the money supply itself is being inflated.

During a recession people wisely stop spending. When they do, demand drops and prices should fall. But sometimes these forces are counterbalanced by an expanding money supply that diminishes the value of currency. When inflation is present in a recession, prices may go up (if the printing is fast enough), stay flat, or fall less than they would have with no inflation.

But during a recession prices need to fall in order to rebalance the economy. Recessions should be deflationary. Falling prices will cushion the blow of low employment. Somehow, modern economists see falling prices as a never-ending abyss toward demand destruction. They forget that when prices fall far enough, people start spending again. The process allows unneeded inventories to be worked off, and for prices to fall to a level justified by underlying supply and demand.

By keeping prices artificially high, inflation prevents this from happening.

CHAPTER
11

A LIFELINE
FROM AFAR

When the senators convened, Greenfin told them that there was nothing more he could do: the bank was simply out of fish. Some senators suggested that they tell the truth to the islanders. Those proposals died in committee. Lindy searched for better answers.

He asked the island's brilliant economist Ben Barnacle to take over at the bank.

"No problem, sir," said Barnacle. "The situation is that the citizens are losing confidence. If we can start spending more of our Fish Reserve Notes now, that will restore confidence and then the citizens will start spending again. If I have to, I'll drop the Fish Reserve Notes from palm trees."

Some of the senators were a bit confused. Although none of them had Barnacle's economic training, some had the feeling that the problems stemmed from spending too much to begin with. Buddy Goldfish tried to talk some sense, but no one would listen.

Fortunately, the tough choices were avoided by a neat twist of fate.

Suddenly, the Senate door was flung open and one of the island's far-flung ambassadors, barged into the chamber with some very strange-looking people.

The ambassador had discovered an island across the eastern sea called Sinopia, where all the citizens still fished entirely by hand. Lacking the benefits of a free and developed economy, Sinopia struggled under the autocratic rule of an all-powerful king, who had subjected his people to whimsical experiments in social structure.

In Sinopia, all citizens were required to fish, but their catch did not belong to them. Instead fish were turned over to the king, who then decided which subjects deserved to get some back.

When the Sinopian king noticed that the diligence of some of the fishermen began to lag, he decided to require them all to sing together patriotically while they fished. Those who forgot the words, or hit a sour note, would not be fed until they learned how to carry the tune.

Although this system did not produce much fish per capita, those in control did take a very significant portion of what was caught. So while the king and his court dined on ocean delicacies, the average Sinopian got by on half of a fish per day.

Much like Usonia before the first development of capital, Sinopia had no savings, no bank, no credit, and no business. From the Usonian perspective, the Sinopian economy was still stuck in the dark ages.

To his credit, the Sinopian king was savvy enough to realize that his island was going nowhere fast. Upon hearing the tales of Usonia, the king was impressed by the luxurious lifestyle of its citizens, as well as the island's advanced system of banking, credit, and commerce. He was determined to bring the same level of prosperity to his island.

After observing how the oceanwide economy functioned, the king surmised that possession of Fish Reserve Notes was the key to advancement.

Indeed, he was aware that the notes were used as money across the entire ocean. The Bongobians accepted Fish Reserve Notes as payment for their bongos, and the Dervishers took them in exchange for their coconut oil products.

Sensing that the possession of the notes would allow his island greater access to the transoceanic economy, the Sinopian ambassador offered to exchange fish caught by his citizens for Fish Reserve Notes.

The senators looked at the Sinopians in disbelief. Then they looked at each other in giddy wonder. Could it be so easy? Access to fresh fish…in exchange for pieces of paper?

Without hesitation, Lindy B. stepped forward and agreed to their terms. Usonia would generously open the island's markets to Sinopian fish imports…and by the way, when could they start unloading the fish?

But before they drew up the paperwork, the Sinopian ambassador asked for reassurance that Fish Reserve Notes would always have real value.

"No worries," said Lindy B. "Anytime you want real fish for those notes, you just mosey up to our bank's fish window and we'll be happy to give you whatever you need. Just take a look around…does it look like we're short of fish?"

The treaty was signed and the Sinopian fish were delivered. In exchange, Lindy handed over a couple of stacks of freshly printed notes. Barely containing a chuckle he offered some parting advice, "Be careful with these, fellas. These things are very hard to come by."

Turning to the head banker, he said, "Hey Barnacle, let's get these fish over to the bank before we open for business."

The relieved bank president needed no convincing. "No problem, sir. I've got a team of fish technicians waiting in the vault. They're ready to slice and dice these babies as soon as they arrive. All the depositors will get their fish today. And unlike yesterday, there will be plenty of meat on the bones!"

And so a new chapter in Usonia's economic history was born. Every day brought a new cargo canoe from Sinopia to make a deposit of fish, and every day the Sinopians got a new pile of Fish Reserve Notes in exchange.

The major question for the Sinopians was what to do with all the notes. The best thing would be to trade them for goods made by the Usonians. Of course, the Sinopians needed nets to increase their fishing efficiency, and Usonian manufacturers made the best nets in the ocean. So, the Able Net Company landed a massive order.

After all their buying, the Sinopians had some Fish Reserve Notes left over. Given the lack of a banking system in their home island, they decided to leave this trade surplus on deposit at the Fish Reserve Bank, where it would at least earn some interest.

The transactions were a huge boom to Usonia. Not only did the foreign demand boost the local economy, but deposits of Sinopian fish at the bank swelled the availability of credit. Even though the Usonians were spending more than they saved, there was still plenty of fish available to lend at low rates of interest.

With plenty of real fish to add meat to the
bones of official fish, Usonia's problem of
fishlation largely disappeared.
With plumper fish, prices
stopped rising and living
standards rose once again.

In Sinopia things
changed rapidly as well.

The Sinopian king belatedly realized
the fatal flaw in his domestic economic
model. His islanders simply would not fish if they had to
give up all that they caught. Knowing this, the king made
a dramatic reversal in policy when the nets came in from
Usonia. Those who purchased nets from the king could
keep all the extra fish they caught. Not surprisingly, this
resulted in an increase in the Sinopians' daily fishing
activities.

But there was a hitch — in order to facilitate greater trans-
island trade, the king required his citizens to swap their extra
fish for Fish Reserve Notes.

With personal incentives finally in place, it didn't take
long for the Sinopians to accumulate savings and expand
production. As a result, Sinopian entrepreneurs were now
able to build factories to make other goods, like spoons and
bowls. And even though most Sinopians still lacked these
things, they sold these goods back to Usonians, for, you
guessed it, more Fish Reserve Notes.

TAKEAWAY

For years, economists have mischaracterized the relationship between the United States and China. Most see it as a mutually beneficial system whereby the United States gets cheap products and cheap loans, and China gets manufacturing jobs. But is such an arrangement really a benefit for both parties?

The Americans do well: they get stuff without producing it and they get to borrow money without having to save. For their part, the Chinese get to work without consuming what they produce.

They save, but they don't get to borrow. Where's the benefit there?

Most contemporary economic pundits also fail to appreciate the degree to which low interest rates in the United States are made possible by high savings rates abroad. Remember, in order to lend, someone has to save. Fortunately for the United States, the global economy allows these relationships to go beyond borders.

The trump card for the United States thus far has been the status of the U.S. dollar. As the world's official *reserve*, the dollar is accepted as the exchange currency for any international transaction. This means that everyone, not just the United States and its trading partners, needs dollars to conduct trade. So even if no one actually buys things that are made in this country, dollars are always in demand. No other country has this monetary good fortune.

Many of these dollars held by foreigners are typically deposited in American banks, where they can be borrowed by Americans. That way we can spend even if we don't save.

By holding their currency to a strict peg against the U.S. dollar, the Chinese authorities have essentially required that their citizens hold at least some of their savings in U.S. dollars.

Without these savings from China and other nations, everyone in the United States including the government would have a much more difficult time borrowing, and they would likely have to pay much higher interest rates for the privilege. High interest rates and scarce credit would be a lethal combination for our debt-fueled economy.

As current American leaders come into increasing conflict with China, this lifeline needs to be clearly understood, before it is callously cast adrift. Of course, since this relationship cannot last forever, the sooner it ends the less painful it will be, particularly for Americans. The longer you eat for free, the harder it is to feed yourself when the free food stops coming.

12

THE SERVICE SECTOR STEPS UP

With the influx of Sinopian savings pushing down interest rates, Usonian entrepreneurs descended on bank loan officers with their best business ideas. But as the jobs of fishing and producing became increasingly outsourced to the Sinopians, the business plans they presented were very different from what the bank had seen in prior generations. Most business proposals now favored companies that required local workers to deliver a service. These jobs could not be outsourced and were generally less capital intensive.

In a celebrated oration given at the island's first economic conference, Ben Barnacle explained the changes. He argued that the Usonian economy had developed to the point where the lowly process of fishing and production could be relegated to poorer economies, leaving Usonians free to pursue more sophisticated "service sector" jobs like chefs, storytellers, tattoo artists, and the like.

Evidence of this change could be seen at Charlie Surfs, the venerable surfboard shop established by one of the island's founders.

After generations of manufacturing success, the company was moving in a new direction. Charlie's descendants landed a big loan to vastly expand their surfing school operations. Twelve new gleaming campuses were built across the island.

At the same time, the company struck a deal to manufacture its boards in Sinopia, paying off the foreign workers with Fish Reserve Notes, The higher-value activities of surfboard design and surfing instruction remained at home.

Soon more service sector businesses began to take root. The manufacturing facilities that had once populated the island began to be replaced by retail operations that sold goods primarily made on other islands.

The outsourcing trend was accelerated by various regulations, fees and taxes imposed by the Senate to make businesses cater to voters concerns. These obstacles made it harder for Usonian businesses to compete in the new trans-ocean economy.

Meanwhile, across the ocean, Sinopia was being transformed as well....

As expected, the imported net technology, combined with the energizing power of self-interest, caused fishing productivity to soar. Eventually Sinopians saved enough to build numerous mega-fish catchers of their own (the copyright infringement lawsuit brought by the original designers went nowhere in the Sinopian courts). They implemented a 24-hour fishing policy, with three shifts cranking out fish nonstop. A good portion of these fish were exported to Usonia.

As fish production became more efficient, workers were freed up for other tasks, most notably, manufacturing. Since the king's policy involved the accumulation of Fish Reserve Notes, he mandated that most of this new capacity be devoted to products that could be exported.

As canoe load after canoe load of fish and goods headed across the sea to Usonia, a flood of Fish Reserve Notes headed in the opposite direction.

In a typical trade relationship (like the one
between Bongobia and Dervishia),
Sinopian goods would have
been exchanged for
Usonian goods that
were in demand
back in Sinopia.
But the Sinopian
willingness
to accumulate
notes produced a
completely different
relationship in
which one island
largely produced and
the other consumed.

Why the Sinopian king would tolerate such an arrangement
puzzled many. But in comparison to some of his earlier
schemes, this one seemed downright logical. The policy kept
the king firmly in control, but it was hardly a boon to the

Sinopians who made surfboards but were too busy working to ever surf themselves.

Of course, the Sinopians believed that their ultimate reward would come in the future, when they could stop fishing and live off their savings of Fish Reserve Notes. Little did they realize that Usonia lacked the fishing capacity to feed its own citizens, let alone make good on all its outstanding notes.

At another island economic conference, Ben Barnacle claimed that this system represented the newest and most efficient example of economic specialization.

✔ REALITY CHECK

Like most economists of his generation, Barnacle saw consumption as the elusive driving force of growth. The biggest consumers were therefore considered the engines of growth.

But shopping in a mall is much more pleasurable than working in a mill. Anyone with half a brain knows that.

He explained that Usonia had a comparative advantage in consuming, and that this capacity was a great benefit to the entire ocean. No other island, he argued, had citizens of such voracious appetites, who could always be relied on to demand more. Usonians' wide roads, big carts, and big huts made them the most efficient consumers!

The optimistic, can-do spirit of Usonia also meant that its citizens never feared to spend...even when they didn't have two guppies to rub together. As a result, other islands could efficiently outsource consumption to Usonia!

On the flip side, Barnacle explained that the Sinopians were considered the best at generating savings and manufacturing products. Therefore, he argued, "It is simply more efficient to outsource production to Sinopia."

TAKEAWAY

Over the past decade, the problem of global imbalances has been a perennial topic at all the most important economic events. But despite the speeches and the acres of newsprint devoted to the topic, there has been absolutely no progress made toward resolving the problem.

The most visible statistic that charts the phenomenon is the U.S. trade deficit. For most of our history the United States exported much more than it imported, resulting in trade surpluses. In some years, especially toward the middle of the twentieth century, these surpluses were truly massive. We used the excess funds to build more capital at home, and to buy up more capital abroad. In the process we became the richest country on the planet. But in the late 1960s the trade balance started to change, and by 1976 the United States began running persistent trade deficits.

The dollar's reserve status has played a significant role in allowing this deficit to grow unchecked. Without the built-in demand for dollars made possible by the global economic system, no country could long sustain such imbalances. Companies and governments would simply refuse to trade goods for a currency with which it couldn't buy anything.

During the 1970s and 1980s these deficits were on the magnitude of $10 billion to $50 billion per year—large, but manageable. In the 1990s, the figures started hitting the $100 billion mark. Although the extras digits were alarming, the gap was still relatively small in comparison to our massive economy. But with the new millennium, things started to get silly.

For the first decade of the twenty-first century, which corresponded with the rise of China as an export economy, the U.S. trade deficit averaged around $600 billion per year, topping out at a staggering $763 billion in 2006. That's more than $2,500 for every man, woman, and child in the United States.

After the recession of 2008 began, those figures mercifully started to retreat. But as we will see, U.S. policies soon put an end to that positive reversal.

Normally, trade deficits tend to be self-correcting.

A country with a trade surplus, in that it sells more abroad than it buys, will create an international demand for its currency. If you want its stuff, you need its currency. As a result, strong trading positions tend to strengthen a country's currency. The opposite is true with countries with weak trading positions. If no one wants your stuff, no one really needs your currency.

But when a country's currency rises, its products become more expensive. This gives a competitive opportunity to countries with weak currencies to start selling some of their products into that market. When they sell more, demand for their currencies rises. This currency counterweight should keep runaway trade imbalances in check.

But the dollar's reserve status, and the decision of the Chinese government to maintain the currency peg, has gummed up the machinery and has allowed the situation to grow dangerously out of kilter.

CHAPTER
13
CLOSING THE FISH WINDOW

Eventually, as Fish Reserve Notes continued to pour out of Usonia and pile up on islands throughout the ocean, some foreign holders began questioning the ability of Usonia to redeem them with actual fish.

Chuck DeBongo, the charismatic leader of the Bongobians, gained favor at home by deriding the arrogance and power of Usonia. Believing that the acceptance of Fish Reserve Notes was unnecessarily enhancing Usonia's economic power, he started to send more and more of his financial agents to the bank's fish window to exchange his notes for real fish.

When those withdrawals started to make a real impact on the fish reserves, the technicians had to get busy again. As they sliced and diced, official fish once again became noticeably smaller, causing fishflation to rear its slimy head.

Consequently, the island's economy deteriorated once again.

The new Senator-in-Chief, Slippery Dickson, was told by his economic advisors that if other islands followed the Bongobians' lead, an oceanwide run on the Fish Reserve Bank could empty the vault of fish and wipe out the value of the notes.

Barnacle and the senators started to worry.

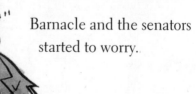

Lacking the spine to ask for tough choices from his citizens, Slippie (as he was known), decided to pin the losses on foreigners. He took the bold step of closing the bank's fish window to foreign depositors! From now on, the value of Fish Reserve Notes on the international market would be determined only by what someone was prepared to trade for them, not because they could be redeemed for fish. In truth, the notes' value would hang on Usonia's status as a great economic and military power.

The breaking of the "fish standard" caused many islands around the ocean to lose confidence in the notes. Not surprisingly, their value dropped sharply. But as they were still the most common form of money across the ocean, the fall eventually stabilized. Fortunately for the Usonian Senate, the closing of the fish window allowed the currency crisis to pass without bringing on a regime-changing catastrophe (the only real danger as far as the senators were concerned). Slippie breathed a sigh of relief.

Chuck DeBongo fumed and made threatening speeches. But his efforts proved largely symbolic — Usonia's power was unassailable.

Unfortunately, Slippie himself was later brought down by the subsequent Watersnake Scandal, in which he was caught with a large cache of stolen reptiles.

With the currency crisis in the past, fishflation largely under wraps, and Fish Reserve Notes maintaining their status despite the closing of the fish window,

the Usonian economy settled down. A few years later, a boost toward prosperity was provided by the election of Roughy Redfish to Senator-in-Chief.

Roughy succeeded in lowering taxes, rolling back some burdensome regulations, and reducing barriers to free trade with other islands. However, he failed in his promise to reduce government spending. Despite the favorable business climate he instilled, the difference between what the Senate spent and what it raised in taxes continued to grow. In fact, under Roughy's watch, the gap widened dangerously.

Fortunately, fresh fish from foreign sources continued to roll into the bank. The notes that were used to pay for these fish were exported and never redeemed for actual fish. With such a favorable dynamic in place, Usonia set sail into what appeared to be an era of unprecedented prosperity.

TAKEAWAY

From the beginning of recorded history, humanity has used all sorts of things as money. Salt, shells, beads, livestock—all had their day. But over time metals, particularly gold and silver, have emerged as the most widely used forms of money. This is not an accident. Precious metals have all the qualities that make money valuable and useful: scarcity, desirability, uniformity, durability, and malleability.

Even if people didn't want the metal as money, it still had value based on its other uses and relative scarcity.

In contrast, paper money has value only as long as enough people agree to take it in exchange for goods and services. But that makes its value completely subjective. Since it can be produced at will, and has no intrinsic value itself, the paper can become worthless if enough people lose faith in it.

Although economists talk like they have seen it all before, the truth is humanity simply has no long-term precedent for universal economic activity based on irredeemable paper money.

History can show us many episodes in which individual governments, out of fiscal desperation, hitched their wagons to worthless currencies. Those experiments always ended in grief, especially for the citizens of the offending country.

That's because it is impossible for one country to sustain a worthless currency while its neighbors continue to issue real money. Naturally, foreigners would refuse to take the worthless currency, and eventually a black market for real money would arise in the country itself.

But now we are in a "through the looking glass" world where, for the past 40 years, no country issues real money. This is the biggest monetary experiment ever conducted. No one knows how or when it will end. But rest assured, it will.

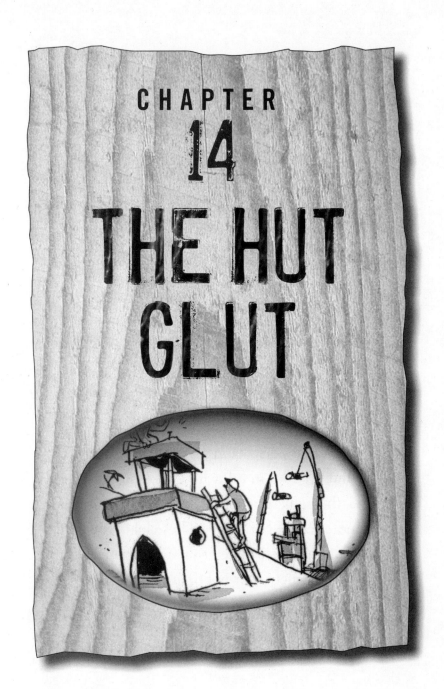

CHAPTER
14
THE HUT
GLUT

Despite the success achieved by Charlie Surfs' switch to the service sector, bank loan officers remained somewhat leery about providing funds for risky service sector businesses. Looking for a safe bet, they soon cast their eyes at the island's sleepy hut loan market, which seemed to offer a good source of low-risk loans.

Up until that point, the hut market had never figured prominently into the overall economic picture. The huts themselves were typically modest affairs well suited to the islanders' tropical lifestyle. But with prosperity growing and interest rates low, demand for newer, bigger and better huts began to emerge.

Traditionally, islanders would save for years, and then pay for a hut up front in full with cold, hard fish. But over time, the bank started making hut loans to the island's more secure borrowers. These loans meant that borrowers did not have to defer their purchases and could buy huts whether or not their savings equaled the purchase price.

Although such lending did not expand the island's productive capacity, or increase the borrower's capacity to repay (as a business loan did), these loans did have good underlying security. That was because, unlike a loan made to an entrepreneur with an unproven business idea, a hut loan came with a piece of solid collateral attached...the hut itself. If the borrower couldn't pay back the loan, the bank would take possession of the hut, which it could resell to pay off the loan.

Even with this collateral, there was no guarantee that the bank could get all its money back after such a sale. As a result of this risk, the bank demanded that borrowers come up with a substantial amount of fish for a down payment. This commitment would provide the bank with some assurance that the buyer would continue to pay. It would also limit the bank's losses if the borrower couldn't pay back the entire loan.

Some islanders resented the fact that access to hut loans was unequal. The wealthy usually got loans easily, but those who had no savings or poor credit had a much harder time. Some felt that the poor were being denied access to the island's upper echelons of wealth. Sensing a potent campaign issue, the Senate got into the game to fix the problem.

Arguing that hut ownership lay at the very core of the Usonian Dream, Senator Cliff Cod devised a plan where the government would ensure that everyone could get a hut loan. Not only would the Senate mandate ultra-low interest rates with very low down payment requirements, but it would stand behind the loans and pay the bank back if the borrower couldn't.

In order to facilitate the process, Cod created two agencies—Finnie Mae and Fishy Mac—to buy hut loans from the bank. The hut buyer would then pay back the agencies directly. The bank would immediately get back its principal, which it could use to make new loans (and be rewarded with a generous fee for its efforts). With the Senate guarantees in place, the bank dropped interest rates as it no longer needed the extra revenue to protect itself from losses due to defaulting loans.

The hut lending program was a huge hit with the bank, which was able to make nearly risk-free profits. It was also popular among voters, who no longer had to save half their lives to buy a hut. Based on his shrewd maneuvering, Cod was rewarded with a nearly lifetime Senate term.

Another agency, Sushi Mae, was devised to underwrite loans for youngsters wishing to enroll in surfing school. Guaranteed tuition loans on the table enticed more and more islanders to brush up on their cutbacks and nose riding.

With easy access to Sushi Mae loans, Charlie Surfs was able to raise tuition rates aggressively, without worrying about pricing its customers out of the market. Soon, tuitions began rising much faster than the overall rate of fishflation. Most economists assumed that the higher prices simply reflected the increasing social value of a surfing degree.

To keep pace with tuition increases, Sushi Mae continually increased the size of loans it was willing to guarantee. In a few years, surfing school tuition became one of life's most daunting costs.

Similarly, with Finnie and Fishy on the job, the island's hut building, hut selling, and hut decorating industries took off. These activities sucked up more and more of the island's productive energy, without doing much to bring in any more actual fish or increasing anyone's ability to repay hut loans.

✔ REALITY CHECK

Although these loan policies appeared to be a win-win for all involved, in truth, the system created great dangers. The Senate had distorted the credit market by imposing incentives that favored hut loans and education loans over other loans that had no guarantees. Loans were now being made not because they were necessarily the best use of savings, but because the senators had a political stake in encouraging hut ownership and education.

As interest rates for hut loans dropped due to the Finnie and Fishy guarantees, islanders were able to take out bigger loans. As a result, just like surfing school tuition, hut prices started moving noticeably higher. With steady price increases, islanders began to perceive hut ownership not just as an expense worth shouldering but as a vital investment. To guarantee a prosperous future, hut ownership was considered better than saving.

The Senate further stimulated the hut sector by declaring that profits made from buying and selling huts would be largely tax free, and that interest paid for hut loans could be deducted from the yearly fish tax. As a result, looking to buy and sell a hut for profit became a much more bankable financial plan than trying to start a business or saving for the future. Not surprisingly, the island got more new huts. But it also got less savings and fewer new businesses.

When the pace of hut price increases really gathered steam, loan amounts bumped into the limits that the Senate had placed on Finnie and Fishy loans. When that happened, Senator Cod inevitably stepped in, declared the fundamental soundness of both institutions, and urged the Senate to increase loan limits so that huts could remain affordable. He always prevailed.

The head honchos at Finnie and Fishy, both old friends of Cod, rewarded the senator's efforts with generous contributions to his reelection campaign and a sweetheart loan on his own hut.

Given that Finnie and Fishy paid a higher rate of interest to its investors than did the Fish Reserve Bank, the Sinopians piled some of their surplus fish notes into Finnie and Fishy.

They took confidence from the fact that the Senate
seemed to stand behind the solvency
of the two lending
institutions.

The influx of Sinopian investment fish into the hut loan
market swelled the availability of credit and brought down
interest rates even further. This meant bigger loans became
even more affordable. In turn, the ease of getting a big loan
allowed buyers to throw caution into the wind and bid up hut
prices even higher.

Sensing the profit potential, Manny Fund VII jumped
into the market with both feet. The descendant of the
island's first venture capitalist noticed that there were
some loans that were so ridiculously risky that even Finnie
and Fishy wouldn't touch them. But given the mania
for hut investment, he believed he could rely on the old
Manny Fund panache to convince buyers that the loans
were solid.

Manny began offering islanders a new type of loan, which he called "hut fish extractions," in which hut owners replaced existing mortgages with bigger loans on the huts that they already owned. The new financing would pay back the original loan and put the extra fish into the borrower's pocket. The rise in hut prices justified the bigger loans. With Manny's "fish-traction" loans, anyone who owned a hut could get his hands on essentially free fish!

With the relatively high interest that Manny charged to fish-traction borrowers, his investment fund was able to offer even better yields to its investors. Not wanting to be left out of the party, Fishy and Finnie asked Cod to let them buy these riskier, higher-rate loans as well. When the approval came through, the two agencies became the biggest lenders in the fish-traction market.

Fish equity extractions provided a huge shot in the arm to the hut improvement industry, which became a major focus of economic activity. Hut Depot, an islandwide chain selling primarily imported hut improvement paraphernalia, employed dozens of specialists to show the islanders how to make more money through the magic of hut improvement. It was widely accepted that every fish spent on hut improvement would result in two fish in higher sales prices. No one was really sure why this was so…but why question the professionals?

Huts became much more luxurious than ever before. Fire pits were lined with polished abalone shells; water buckets were pulled aloft on the finest silk ropes. Many huts were fitted with designer thatchings and came with built-in wide-screen windows.

Soon islanders began demanding not just primary hut residences, but also investment and vacation huts. Some islanders even built vacation huts on top of their regular huts.

But then a strange thing happened. With all the demand for huts created by fish-traction loans, low (or no) down payment requirements, tax-free profit policies, and all the fish showered on borrowers by the bank as a result of the Finnie and Fishy guarantees, hut prices really started to go wild. Prices had always gone up a few percentage points every year, but now they were going up by that much every month! Bidding wars broke out for even the dumpiest huts.

Things got to the point where traditional measures of affordability no longer applied. It used to be that islanders would pay no more than two or three times their yearly

income for a hut. Now they were paying 10 or 20 times.
People bought huts that they knew they could not afford
in the belief that they could sell in a few years for far
more than they paid. With that kind of profit potential,
no downside risk, and oodles of government incentives
including subsidized loans at artificially low interest rates,
nobody could resist.

But the rapid rise in hut prices was a boon to the senators.
The easy riches made voters feel wealthy and provided
circumstantial evidence of wise economic leadership.
Naturally the senators took every effort to keep the merry-
go-round spinning. Ben Barnacle, and even the elaborately
esteemed Ally Greenfin, assured all that there could be no
such thing as a hut glut, because hut prices simply could
not fall.

Not just politicians talked up the mania. The island's
most respected private sector thinkers were the loudest
cheerleaders. The dapper Barry Codroe had a popular stage
show, where islanders discussed current events. The always
optimistic Codroe dubbed the expansive era the "Goldfish
Economy." Regular panelists like Carp Gaffer assured
islanders that hard times were nowhere in sight and that bank
policy had never been better. One occasional guest, Piker
Skiff, often brought in for comic relief, warned of the pending
hut collapse. His foreboding elicited howls of laughter.

TAKEAWAY

Now that it is painfully clear to everyone that the United States experienced the joy and pain of an inflating and collapsing housing bubble, we must take pains to remember that the vast majority of economists, government officials, and financial pundits could not see the calamity coming even as it stared them down at point-blank range.

It was as if all the meteorologists in the country failed to predict a category 5 hurricane when it was just 10 miles off the coast of Miami. Is there any more evidence needed to confirm the utter cluelessness of mainstream economic thinkers?

By any measure of sober valuation, home prices by 2006 had passed into Fantasyland. Valuations were disconnected from every gauge that had been designed to measure their affordability. None of the numbers added up. Yet somehow, economists came up with rationales that seemingly justified the ascent.

But people failed to see the agendas behind the cheerleading. Politicians wanted to keep voter confidence high through a sense of false prosperity; businesses wanted to keep consumers spending on products and services that they really couldn't afford; cable networks wanted to keep ratings high with optimistic hurrahs; and banks, mortgage originators, and real estate brokers wanted to continue making money on fees and interest. All of these interest groups had hired guns who put lipstick on the biggest, ugliest pig imaginable. And amazingly, their explanations were accepted.

So the good news is that now we have finally learned to be more realistic…right? Wrong. Even after the collapse of the mortgage market, people still don't understand how home prices are influenced by government policies. And so while the Bush and Obama administrations have committed massive amounts of government resources to prop up the deflating market, people still don't recognize how these trusses are simply extending the pain and setting us up for an even bigger fall.

CHAPTER
15
THE HUT
RUT

It's hard to say when the market first turned. Perhaps it was the high-profile demise of the Crater View Condominium Huts, which, despite their amenities, ample square footage, and unmatched ocean and lava views, somehow failed to attract buyers.

As Manny Fund was the principal underwriter of the project, the investment company took a big hit when the developer defaulted on the construction loan. When nervous real estate investors saw the losses at the Crater View Condos, many of them took a hard look at some of their other risky real estate holdings. A distinct apprehension began to spread.

Soon, buyers—both large and small—figured the market had peaked. Many decided that they should sell their current properties, take their frothy profits, and wait for a more favorable time to reinvest.

There was just one problem—everyone was thinking the same thing at the same time. Most of the owners in the market never intended to hold their properties very long to begin with. So when the market began to turn, everybody wanted out. In short order, the island was awash with sellers and devoid of buyers. When that happened, the unthinkable occurred—prices didn't just decline in a modest, orderly fashion…they started plummeting. The hut glut had quickly turned into a massive hut rut.

Suddenly, hut ownership, once a surefire ticket to easy wealth, became a decidedly riskier proposition. With prices no longer rising, huts did not create any fish equity to extract and profits from quick resales were no longer possible. With the pot of gold no longer looming at the end of the rainbow, uncomfortably high loan payments became a burden hardly worth bearing

This situation was further complicated when temporally low introductory teaser rates reset higher, which made the homes instantly unaffordable for those borrowers whose only hope had been a quick resale or fish-traction. With homes worth less than their underlying loans, the temptation to walk away from big payments became intense. This was especially true for those who did not put any fish down at purchase. Having made no prior commitment of funds, these borrowers had nothing to lose by not paying their mortgages and allowing the bank to foreclose.

As more and more borrowers defaulted, Manny Fund's securitized loan business was soon declared bankrupt. The losses overwhelmed the venerable institution. Shortly thereafter both Fishy and Finnie admitted that they too were belly-up.

With consumers no longer extracting hut equity, the industries that grew up around the hut glut also fell into crisis. Hut builders, design consultants, window trimmers, and appliance salespeople werelaid off in droves.

Other seemingly disparate industries were impacted as well. The Usonian donkey cart makers had benefited greatly from hut equity extractions. Effortlessly pulling fish out of their appreciating huts had allowed islanders to buy bigger and bigger carts. In the go-go days, many of these wagons became so large that four or five donkeys were needed to pull them. (This was problematic as most of the donkeys were imported.) With no more hut equity to tap into, sales of these "grass guzzlers" plummeted, and the cart companies fell into bankruptcy.

The island became ensnared in the worst economic crisis since the great monsoon of Franky Deep's era. Growing desperate, the unemployed workers converged on the Senate demanding solutions.

Stimulus to the Rescue

After years of denying any weakness in the economy, the island's Senator-in-chief, George W. Bass, belatedly set to work fixing the problem.

With strong unanimity, his advisors recommended bold incentives that would get consumers spending again, especially on huts. Without any understanding of why savings and production fuel economic growth, the Senate decided on a program of bailouts and stimuli.

Their first rescue was for Finnie and Fishy, which were taken over by the Senate directly and were stocked with new Fish Reserve Notes to cover their losses. The reorganized companies were ordered by their new management (the Senate) to offer ultra-low-rate hut loans to anyone who had the wherewithal to fill out an application.

It was hoped that the continued availability of easy credit would increase demands for huts, and thereby stop the slide in prices.

When these policies failed to stem the fall, Bass called an emergency meeting of his top advisors, including Ben Barnacle, who had previously assured him that prosperity would be endless.

"Hey, Barney," said the Senator-in-Chief in his trademark folksy demeanor. "You sure sold me a bill of goods on this one. I thought this economy thing was supposed to be simple. You know, they make 'em, we eat 'em, and everyone gets a hut or two! I mean how do we get the shark to smell the chum on this one?"

The other senators searched for the meaning of his metaphor. Perhaps none existed.

"Well, sir, the problem is quite simple," said Hank Plankton, the new head fish accountant. "Hut prices are falling, so citizens don't feel as wealthy as they did before. As a result, they have stopped spending. If we can push hut prices back up, people will start spending again."

"Cool, Plankie, I knew this was gonna be a breeze," said Bass. "How we gonna do that? Do we have someone in charge of that? Sounds like a cool job. Maybe I'll appoint one of my biggest donors."

"Well, sir, it's not quite that simple," said Plankton. "We can't just mandate that hut prices go back up. As you know, we have kept Finnie and Fishy lending. Unfortunately, that alone is not enough. For some reason the people don't want to borrow. Perhaps the loan application is still too complicated. But for now, we need to push interest rates lower and then give people more tax breaks to buy huts. That should create a lot of demand for loans, which should stop hut prices from falling and get hut builders busy again."

✔ REALITY CHECK

The last thing the island needed was more huts. There were already too many huts. Any energy or resources spent building more huts would be wasted.

Similarly, hut prices were still too high. They had been bid up to ridiculous levels by a combination of factors that would never return. Trying to keep them from falling was like trying to keep a bridge from collapsing after all the supports had been knocked away.

Despite the fact that many islanders were upset for overpaying for their huts, the island economy would actually be better off if hut prices came down and building ceased altogether, at least until real demand returned. That way people could spend less on huts and have more to spend on things the economy lacked—like new businesses and carts that could be pulled by just one donkey. Resources used for new hut construction, like bamboo and rope, could be used for new businesses instead.

Unfortunately, government interventions would prevent this natural reallocation of resources from occurring.

Plankton continued laying out his plans. "We also need to make sure that Manny Fund remains solvent. The company owes a lot of fish to a lot of people. If it were to go down, the entire island economy would utterly collapse. We also need to make sure that no one who invested in Manny Fund loses any fish. If we don't do this, I'm sure that we would all starve… especially the children."

"Well, that aint gonna happen on my watch, Plankie," replied Bass. "Tell them that we're gonna come to the rescue with a bailout. Hey, didn't you used to work there?"

"Yes, Mr. Senator, I was the president of the company. But I really don't see how that has any relevance to this conversation, and frankly, I resent the insinuation."

"Aw heck, Hank, I was just funnin," Bass continued. "Okay. After we get hut prices back up, and keep Manny and the boys in business, how are we gonna get people spending again? Where they gonna get the fish? I mean last time I checked, we were all a bit tapped in the tuna department. Isn't that why they're outside holding pitchforks?"

"Well, sir, we plan on distributing new Fish Reserve Notes to all the citizens. That should get them spending."

"That's cool. But where we gonna get the fish? Haven't our technicians stretched the sturgeons about a far as they can?"

"Well, sir, we have some new commitments from the Sinopians. They have offered to buy the Water Works system for 100,000 fish."

"Hold on honcho. Sell the Water Works? You're talking about jeopardizing our national security! They'd have me tarred and feathered for giving up something like that to those carpetbaggers. Couldn't they just make it a loan instead?"

After months of tense negotiations, Bass's ambassadors convinced the Sinopians that a sale of the Water Works was politically impossible. Instead, the Sinopians somewhat bitterly agreed to make a 100,000-fish loan.

"Hey, Hank," said Bass, after word came back of the successful outcome. "Great news, we got the loan. Just one thing. How are we gonna pay it back?"

"Well, sir, I expect that we will just print up another batch of Fish Reserve Notes. But this time we will use our very best paper."

"Yeah, but what if they won't take them? Aren't we getting a lot of guff from them people already about the value of our notes? It's like that Chuck DeBongo guy a few years back. Won't they just start selling if we issue so many more notes?"

"Highly unlikely, sir. Think about how many Fish Reserve Notes they already have. If they stop taking them, those notes will lose even more value. We've got them over a barrel. And if things get dicey, we'll just remind them of our 'Strong Fish Policy!'"

"Oh, yeah. I forgot about that. It's nice having that one in your back pocket. Is that where we go out and catch more fish to back up our notes?"

"No sir," chimed Ben Barnacle. "The Strong Fish Policy is all about tone. We don't actually do anything. We just say 'Strong Fish Policy' really clearly and loudly again and again. Also, it helps if you clench your fist and beat it on the table when you say the words."

"Right you are, Barney. Let's just say I know a little something about acting tough. Mission accomplished! Now let's go surfin'!"

TAKEAWAY

I t's hard to overstate the impact the housing boom made on the economy as a whole. During the height of the mania, the financing, construction, and furnishing of homes had become the central dynamo of the U.S. economy. And while everyone acknowledged the good fortune, few spared much concern about the future costs.

In addition to the profits made by real estate "flippers" (those who serially bought and sold properties), homeowners extracted hundreds of billions of dollars per year from their homes. The process turned houses into tax-free ATM machines. People used the money to renovate their homes, take vacations, pay for college, buy cars and electronics, and just generally live better than they would have if their homes had not appreciated in value.

But the wealth was simply a mirage.

In his book *Irrational Exuberance* economist Robert Shiller determined that in the 100 years between 1900 and 2000, home prices in the United States increased by an average of 3.4 percent per year (which is just slightly higher than the average rate of inflation). There were good reasons for this. Prices were firmly tied to people's ability to pay, which is a function of income and credit availability.

But from 1997 to 2006 national home prices gained an astounding 19.4 percent per year on average. Over that time incomes barely budged. So why could people pay so much? The difference was credit, which government policy made much cheaper and easier to get. But credit could not expand forever, and eventually conditions tightened. When they did, there was nothing to hold prices up.

So when the market crested, the easy money that for years had poured into the economy stopped flowing. Even if there had been no other economic reversals that followed the housing bust (which there were), the economy would have had to shrink without all the free cash. A recession was not only inevitable but absolutely necessary to rebalance the economy.

But when the economy started to contract, lawmakers and economists treated the development not as the inevitable consequence of years of easy money and overspending, but as the problem itself. In other words, they mistook the cure for the disease.

The policy goals of both the Bush and Obama administrations have been to encourage consumers to spend as they had before the housing crash. But where will the money come from? If unemployment rose, and incomes and home prices fell, where would consumers get the money?

Economists have declared that if the people can't spend, the government needs to step up and do it for them. But the government doesn't have any money. All it has is what it collects in taxes and what it borrows or prints.

For now, this process is just creating massive public debt ($1.6 trillion per year and counting). And although the numbers look bad, we are still able to sell most of this debt on the open market, primarily to foreigners.

But our "good fortune" can't last forever. Ultimately the U.S. government will have only two options: default (tell our creditors that we can't pay, and negotiate a settlement) or inflate (print money to pay off maturing debt). Either option will lead to painful consequences. Default, which does offer the possibility of a real reckoning and a fresh beginning, is actually the better alternative. Unfortunately, while inflation is worse, it is also the more politically expedient.

CHAPTER
16
STEPPING
ON THE GAS

CARP FOR CARTS
TRADE IN
CENTER

Despite the bailouts and incentives made by Bass and Plankton, the Usonian economy continued to deteriorate during the Great Hut Rut. Strangely, no one showed much interest in buying new huts. Instead of spending their stimulus fish, some islanders elected to save them. With spending stagnant, the cart companies teetered on the edge of extinction. Hut Depot was devastated. Unemployment got worse. Public dissatisfaction intensified.

The next election proved to be pivotal. Barry Ocuda, a candidate for Senator-in-Chief, accused the Bass faction of inadequacy in the face of a national emergency. He pilloried the Bass moves as trifling half measures. Campaigning on a theme of *transformation*, Ocuda promised much greater government efforts to turn the island's economy around.

Taking power, the young Senator-in-Chief got to work, and transformed the Bass policies by tripling them in size! He devised a number of new programs to push newly printed Fish Reserve Notes into the economy.

He increased the amount of assistance that the government would give to hut buyers—initially just to first-time hut buyers and then to trade-up buyers as well. And, once again, he lowered the interest rates that Finnie and Fishy charged.

Noticing that the surfing school attendance had fallen off dramatically, he increased direct aid to schools, and made student loans even easier to get.

He authorized the building of a new lighthouse at Shady Swamp. When engineers pointed out that the facility was not entirely needed, Ocuda reminded them that the construction jobs alone would provide a powerful boost to the economy.

Ocuda, also placed much faith in the need to develop alternative energy sources. He argued, "Society has become too dependent on donkeys. Llamas are far better suited to the island's climate and topography. Not only do llamas consume less grass, but they are far surer footed, have better dispositions, and reproduce with more frequency than traditional donkeys. To top it all off, llama manure is far less offensive to the senses."

Ocuda envisioned a multistage plan to transform the old economy.

First, he would hasten the adoption of llama-based infrastructure through massive stimulus spending. To this end, he called for an aggressive state-run llama breeding program. He also mandated that manufacturers (now run by the Senate directly) redesign and refit the carts for llama use. Last, he set about resurfacing all the island's cart paths with a topsoil better suited for llama feet.

Second, Ocuda also came up with the "Carp for Carts" program, which offered government incentives to get people to turn in their grass guzzlers for more fuel-efficient carts. (This was great news to the Sinopian cart companies that made most of the smaller vehicles.)

✔ REALITY CHECK

To many, the positive impact of programs such as Carp for Carts and the jobs created by the Shady Swamp construction project, was taken for granted. It was easy to see how these ideas boosted sales and put people to work.

But as was the case with Senate-financed hut loans, it was far from certain that such spending was the most effective use of the island's resources. In fact, none of these activities did much to expand productive capacity.

Not nearly as evident were the jobs that were destroyed or not created as a result of diverting scarce labor and capital to the activities that the Senate deemed to be important enough to fund.

Through trial and error, market forces would have determined the best use for remaining investment capital. Enterprises that misread the market would lose money and investors would back away. Those that got it right would profit, attract more capital, and expand.

Perhaps efforts would have been better spent building nets, farming equipment, or canoes. The most successful ventures would have been those that most efficiently gave the people what they wanted, when they wanted it. But with the free market now apparently discredited, everyone put their faith in a small group of people to make decisions normally left to the island as a whole.

As Ocuda and his senatorial ally, Nan ShallowSea, prepared to spend piles of newly printed Fish Reserve Notes, there was one small detail that they overlooked: Usonia was completely out of fish. All their planned spending had to be financed from abroad.

Solely as a result of the willingness of foreigners to trade real goods for paper, Usonians had been able to consume more than they produced. As a result, their current choices were simple:

1. Consume less and use the savings to pay back debt.

2. Produce more and sell the extra goods to pay back debt.

3. Borrow more to continue current levels of consumption.

The first two choices involved unpleasant outcomes for Usonians. Either they would be working harder, eating less, or both. The third choice dealt all the sacrifice to foreigners. Not surprisingly, the senators courageously chose to ship the pain abroad. In so doing, they hoped the renewed spending would restore economic health at home.

✔ REALITY CHECK

But remember an economy can't grow because people spend; people spend because an economy grows. This elusive truth was lost to the senators and all their advisors. In the meantime, the newly printed notes created the illusion of improvement.

The unemployed knew that jobs were being created in Sinopia as fast as they disappeared at home. This resulted from Sinopia's Fish Reserve purchases, which pushed up the value of Fish Reserve Notes and made Sinopian products cheap and irresistible. As a result, Ocuda and ShallowSea publicly lobbied for the Sinopians to dial down their purchases, which would allow Fish Reserve Notes to lose value and make Usonian products more competitive.

Of course, no one had any idea how Sinopia could simultaneously lend the fish necessary to finance the spending envisioned by Ocuda while rolling back the Fish Reserve Note purchases that were the means of the funding. No one even bothered to ask the question. Even while they prepared to borrow more than they ever had before, the senators forgot that someone had to do the lending.

Sinopia Wises Up

On the other side of the ocean, the Sinopians were not nearly as enthusiastic about the senators' plans. Things started to get a little unsettled when the workers got wind of how many more real fish they would be asked to devote to buying Fish Reserve Notes.

Most Sinopians were frustrated with working so hard and getting so little. Since their own government did not provide the social safety nets available in Usonia, the average Sinopian saved lots of money just so they would not be hutless and fishless in old age. Everyone worked, no one had a donkey (let alone a cart), and hardly anyone surfed. Even if they did, they usually went four or five to a board.

The Sinopian king was also losing enthusiasm for the arrangement, and was particularly vexed by the staggering spending plans announced by Ocuda. His advisors, many of whom had been students of the great Ally Greenfin, began to worry that their cache of Fish Reserve Notes would lose value if they stopped buying. And if that happened, Usonians would no longer buy as many Sinopian products.

They argued that without Usonia's thunderous demand, their own export factories would shut down, causing unemployment, discontent, and perhaps even protest (which had never been allowed in Sinopia). Caught on the horns of a dilemma, the Sinopian king kept the status quo going and hoped for an answer.

One day, while he was deep in thought and his council of economic advisors was away on a research expedition, a simple peasant slipped past the palace guards and engaged the worried king in conversation.

"My most glorious leader, please forgive the intrusion, but I hear that you have been troubled by thoughts of fish. Perhaps I may be able to help."

"These are great matters involving trade, savings, investment, and planning. What can you know of such things?" thundered the king.

"Very little, I am sure," conceded the peasant. "But I know that in my village, we all make nothing but wooden bowls, which we send across the sea. In exchange, we get paper, which we save for the future. Someday we hope to buy things with the paper, but now there is little. As we send away our bowls, we wonder why we have no bowls ourselves. We still eat our fish off the floor. Most unsanitary. Would it not be simpler if we just made bowls for ourselves? In that way, our work would improve our lives."

"That's absurd," said the king. "Our people would starve without our exports. How else could we run our economy?"

"Well, my king, as I said, we are good at making bowls. And since—under your wise leadership—we are catching so many more fish, all we need is to find someone here at home who would trade their fish for our bowls. Then all of our productivity would stay here, and our people would have more bowls and more food to put in them."

The king was puzzled. "But wait, the Usonians are so much wealthier than we. How can we compete with their citizens to buy the products we make? They can afford to pay more. They have the Fish Reserve Notes."

"Begging Your Majesty's pardon, but I don't see why we need their notes. They have value only because of our fish and our bowls. We have made the products, so of course we can afford them. We just have to stop giving them away for nothing."

Somehow the simplicity of the peasant's
words made a profound impression on
the king and he decided to change
the policy. No more purchases of
Fish Reserve Notes. From now
on Sinopians would trade their
goods only for real fish!

Since he was
uncomfortable with
the fast change that
the peasant seemed
to advocate, the king
decided on a gradual
course. After all, the
king had plenty of
bowls, none of which were
made of wood.

TAKEAWAY

As a result of a few quarters of positive gross domestic product figures, economists now tell us that the Great Recession is over. But with unemployment still more than 10 percent, and underemployment (those who have given up looking or who work only part-time) still more than 17 percent, many Americans would be surprised to hear the good news.

In truth, the Great Recession had begun the painful, but unfinished, work of rebalancing our economy. In 2009 our national savings rate ticked up for the first time in years, and our trade deficit finally began to shrink after its dizzying ascent earlier in the decade. But the Bush and Obama stimulus programs put a stop to this. The creation of ever greater quantities of debt has given us a reprieve from the process of returning to living standards commensurate with our productivity.

But at some point in the foreseeable future, perhaps in the next few years, we will have a very ugly encounter with our debt. Thus far we have dodged the bullet. Unfortunately, due to our growing annual budget deficits and the looming bankruptcies of Social Security and Medicare (caused in part by the demographic shift of retiring baby boomers), the bullets will be coming at us with much higher force and frequency.

Washington has shown absolutely no willingness to confront the problem. The ability to make significant cuts in government spending has never been considered, let alone attempted. In the early days of his tenure, President Obama made a theatrical show of going through the $3 trillion federal budget "line by line" in order to find "wasteful spending." This resulted in a paltry $17 billion in savings, less than one-half of 1 percent of the budget. Even those proposed cuts elicited howls of protest by both Democrats and Republicans.

If our government won't impose financial discipline, then our creditors, most notably China and Japan, eventually must. Although there are many forms in which this discipline could be delivered, the most likely method is that they simply stop buying our debt.

For now they have fallen into the same trap as the Sinopians. Once they realize that the continual extension of credit to a customer that can't pay is a waste of resources, they will change course. At that point they will refocus their productivity on domestic consumers, who will then fully enjoy the fruits of their labor.

For now, despite increased grumbling and calls for international monetary reform, those nations have kept lending. But their stamina can't be everlasting.

With more than 50 percent of our government debt currently sold to foreign governments, who will pick up the slack when they stop buying? With very little domestic savings to tap into, Americans alone won't be able to do it.

When that day comes, we will have two choices: default or inflation. Both options will violently force American living standards downward through lost purchasing power and higher interest rates.

CHAPTER
17

THE FISH
HIT THE FAN

As the daily deliveries of Sinopian fish slowed, things began to change.

When the Sinopians, the biggest buyers of Fish Reserve Notes, reduced their purchases, the supply of notes began to overwhelm demand. When there is more supply then demand, prices have to fall. As Fish Reserve Notes steadily drifted downward in value, no one wanted to be the one left holding the bag. The Bongobians and the Dervishes then joined the Sinopians in limiting their purchases. With plenty of sellers and no buyers, Fish Reserve Notes entered a death spiral.

Stuck with stacks of rapidly depreciating notes that he couldn't sell, the Sinopian king realized that events had moved beyond his ability to control them. Knowing that his island's Fish Reserve Notes would soon be nearly worthless, he prepared his subjects to bite the bullet. At a mass rally he assured them that short-term pain would soon give way to long-term gain.

As expected, the value of Sinopians' savings of Fish Reserve Notes turned out to be a mirage. The Sinopian economy was pushed into disarray as some businesses closed. But as the peasant had predicted, other businesses soon stepped in and used the spare capacity to make things the Sinopians actually needed.

As they had before, the Sinopians still caught fish, made products, and generated savings. Since these were the essential ingredients that caused an economy to grow, there was no reason for Sinopia to fall into crisis. In fact, with more products available at home and more of their savings in their own banks, living standards started to improve. Savings that in the past were locked up in Fish Reserve Notes were instead lent out to local factories to retool for domestic consumption. As more products were produced for local consumers, Sinopian stores suddenly found themselves stocked with goods. Increased inventories meant that prices could come down.

As the peasant had predicted, despite the losses in their doomed stockpiles of Fish Reserve Notes, Sinopia thrived.

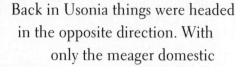

Back in Usonia things were headed in the opposite direction. With only the meager domestic catch available, the bank's fish technicians had to work harder and more creatively than ever before. Official fish began shrinking at an alarming rate and fishflation flared anew. But unlike prior outbreaks, this new variety spiraled out of control.

Soon official fish got so small that they had to be bundled in packages of 50, then 100. Islanders were eating 200 fish a day just to stay alive. Any savings in Fish Reserve Notes became essentially worthless. The condition became known as hyper fishflation.

With fewer products coming in from Sinopia, Usonian retailers were left with diminished inventories. The result of skimpier fish chasing fewer products was soaring prices!

214

Through a rowdy public campaign, the senators attacked retailers for "price gouging." They claimed that fishflation could be stopped if the greedy businesspeople would agree to price controls on products and services. But as these measures focused only on the symptoms of fishflation, rather than the cause, they just made matters worse. Limiting what could be charged for a product without doing anything to control the decreasing value of money simply meant that manufacturers and retailers couldn't make a profit. As a result, they stopped selling and a black market of illegally high-priced merchandise arose.

Sensing the trouble with Fish Reserve Notes, some citizens tried to protect the value of their remaining savings by depositing fish in an offshore bank, where their savings would be protected from senatorial slicing and dicing.

But when the senators noticed this trend, they made it illegal to move savings off the island.

The fear of shrinking fish became so prevalent that no deposits were left in the bank for long. Every fish caught was immediately sliced up and consumed. As had been the case before their economy grew, there were once again no savings, no credit, and no investment.

Unable to come up with any ideas, the senators did what they always did…they discussed plans for the next stimulus. Clearly, the prior attempts to shock the economy back to life were simply too small. The next round would just have to be bigger! However, no one was quite sure what would be used as a stimulant. At this low moment, the mood was lifted by the sight of a Sinopian cargo ship on the horizon.

The senators were thrilled. They assured their fellow islanders that the Sinopians must have seen the errors of their misguided abandonment of Fish Reserve Notes. They would once again be making deposits at the Fish Reserve Bank.

But when the Sinopian ship made port, something entirely different ensued.

Sinopian agents fanned out across the island with wheelbarrows of real fish, and cartloads of Fish Reserve Notes, buying everything, even the stuff that was nailed down. Since no one on Usonia had any real fish anymore, the Sinopians could outbid everybody on everything.

They bought the Water Works, dismantled it, and put it in a cargo canoe. They did the same with the lighthouses. They bought all the donkey carts, surfboards, hand nets, used bongos and even the mega fish catchers. For good measure they snapped up the empty condos so that Sinopian workers could have their own vacation huts.

When their shopping spree was done the Sinopians left, bringing everything of value with them. They left behind the Fish Reserve Notes that they had accumulated over the years. At least, the Usonians would have plenty of kindling for their cooking fires. Finding something to eat was a different matter.

The senators surveyed the devastation and wondered where it had gone wrong. They had spent, so why hadn't the economy grown? Finally it became clear. It was all much simpler than what they had thought.

Addressing an anxious population still looking for answers, Senator Ocuda uttered the most honest words any politician could muster:

"Does anybody here remember how to make a net? I think it's time we all went fishing."

TAKEAWAY

Throughout history, governments have gotten themselves into trouble by spending more than they have. When the gaps become too big, difficult choices arise.

One option is for the government to increase revenue by raising taxes. This path is never popular with citizens, and in a democracy is hard to push through. Even in authoritarian states (where there are no pesky elections), tax increases are problematic. Higher rates always discourage productivity and deflate economic vitality. There is a limit to how high taxes can go. Raise them enough, and people stop working. Raise them higher, and they may even start rioting.

A far better option is to cut government spending. However, this is often more difficult than raising taxes. Those whose benefits are cut are particularly apt to express their hostility both at the polls and on the street. This is especially true when the recipients feel entitled to the benefits. Politicians make lots of promises to secure their elections and voters rarely consider the ability of taxpayers to actually foot the bills.

To avoid either of these politically unpopular options, some governments choose to default instead. In this option a country simply tells its creditors that it can't pay the full amount of its debt obligations. If the debt is largely owed to foreigners, the decision is that much easier to make. Politically speaking, it is better to stiff a foreigner than to raise taxes on, or deny benefits to, a country's own citizens.

For political leaders, default can be rather embarrassing, as it amounts to an official acknowledgment of insolvency. To avoid this, many opt to simply print money to pay debts, effectively repudiating their obligations by inflating them away. Since inflation is usually the easiest choice to make, it is often the most likely. But while it may seem easy at first, it ultimately exacts the harshest toll.

Inflation allows governments to avoid hard choices and dispose of their debt on the sly. By printing money governments can nominally pay back all that they owe, but they do so by diluting their currency. Creditors get paid, but what they get isn't worth much, and if inflation turns into hyperinflation, it's worth nothing.

Inflation is simply a means to transfer wealth from anyone who has savings in a particular currency to anyone who has debt in the same currency. With hyperinflation, the value of savings gets completely wiped out and the burden of debt is removed. (Those who own hard assets do okay, because, unlike savings in currency, assets will rise in nominal value when inflation flares up.)

It has happened many times before: France in the 1790s, the Confederate States of America in the 1860s, Germany in the 1920s, Hungary in the 1940s, Argentina and Brazil in the 1970s and 1980s, and Zimbabwe today. In all of these instances the circumstances that led up to the hyperinflation, and the economic devastation that followed, were remarkably similar. The countries satisfied staggering debt by wiping out the value of their currencies. As a result, their own populations were thrown into abject poverty.

The United States today would certainly be the largest and most advanced economy to ever experience hyperinflation. But that doesn't mean that it can't happen. Thus far our ace in the hole has been the reserve status of the U.S. dollar. This means that the dollar will continue to be widely accepted no matter how bad the fundamentals get. But if we lose reserve status, our currency would be just as vulnerable as those that went down before.

We must look at these possibilities and head them off now, before we no longer have the ability to decide for ourselves.

EPILOGUE

The sorry outcome seen by Usonia in this tale need not be the fate ultimately encountered by that much larger island, the United States of America. Unfortunately, the longer our leaders pursue ever larger doses of the identical policies that were responsible for the financial crisis in the first place, the greater that eventuality becomes.

Although the idea of government stimuli as an antidote to the apparent failures of capitalism was born with Keynes, and nurtured with Roosevelt, it wasn't until Alan Greenspan, George Bush, Ben Bernanke, and Barack Obama that the idea really came into its own. Before 2002, we had never seen federal deficits of this magnitude (now exceeding $1.5 trillion annually), and we had never experimented so radically with ultra low interest rates and manipulation of credit markets.

The mistakes have been so simple, and yet we continue to make them.

In 2002, following the malinvestments of the dot-com era, when billions of dollars were poured into utterly hopeless companies, the economy entered what should have been a protracted downturn. But George Bush, then newly elected, didn't want a bad economy to jeopardize his reelection. So he, and his advisors, dialed up the Keynesian remedies of spending and easy money to an extent not seen for generations.

As a result, the recession of 2002–2003 was one of the shallowest contractions on record. But that benefit came with a heavy long-term cost. The United States ended that recession with greater imbalances than it had before the downturn began. That's not supposed to happen.

Instead of real growth, we kicked off an even bigger asset bubble (in housing) that temporarily overcame the drag of the busted technology bubble. The rising value of housing prices created a great many 'benefits' that masqueraded as economic health. But as we have seen, that vigor was illusory.

The real tragedy is that six years later, when the next crash came, we had failed to learn anything from these mistakes. In diagnosing the causes and prescribing the best cures for the recession of 2008, economists and politicians are getting it dangerously wrong.

In the months since the financial world imploded, a consensus emerged that a lack of adequate regulations brought on the crisis. The roles of government and the Federal Reserve in particular have been largely ignored. As a result, we are getting more of what we don't need (spending and restrictive regulations) and less of what we do (savings and free enterprise).

Wall Street leaders were also irresponsible. The profits made by the big banks during the boom years were obscene. After the crash they should have paid far more dearly than they have. But bankers were playing the distorted hand dealt them by government. Our leaders irrationally promoted home-buying, discouraged savings, and recklessly encouraged borrowing and lending, which together undermined our markets.

Policies enacted by the Federal Reserve, the Federal Housing Administration, Fannie Mae, and Freddie Mac (which were always government entities in disguise), and others created advantages for home buying and selling and removed disincentives for lending and borrowing. The result was a credit and real estate bubble that could only grow — until it could grow no more.

Artificially low interest rates (which made the economy appear healthy) invigorated the market for adjustable-rate mortgages and gave birth to the teaser rate, which made overpriced homes seam affordable. Alan Greenspan himself actively encouraged home buyers to partake. Then government agencies and government-sponsored entities compounded the problem by guaranteeing adjustable-rate mortgages based solely on the ability of borrowers to afford the teaser rates. Without such guarantees most of these mortgages never would have been funded.

Just as prices in a free market are set by supply and demand, financial and real estate markets are governed by the opposing tension between greed and fear. But government has done all that it can to remove fear from the equation.

And so beginning in 2008, as market forces moved to deflate the credit and housing bubbles, the government stepped in to re-inflate both. First came bailouts for Bear Stearns and American International Group (AIG) and guarantees for other Wall Street firms such as Goldman Sachs and Bank of America. Then came Treasury's $700 billion Troubled Asset Relief Program (TARP) to purchase mortgage assets that no one in the private sector would touch. Then the government bailed out student loan provider Sallie Mae and essentially took over the entire student loan market. Bailouts for Detroit automakers soon followed.

Banks and businesses that should have failed were propped up by government support. Capital and labor that should have been freed up to find more productive uses were instead calcified in unneeded activities.

As consumers logically stopped spending after the housing boom deprived them of easy money, the government stepped in with a massive $700 billion stimulus in order to keep the registers ringing. This spending, which the government has borrowed from future generations, has kept us from the pain of living within our means.

By refusing to allow market forces to rein in excess spending, liquidate bad investments, replenish depleted savings, fund capital investment, and help workers transition from the service sector to the manufacturing sector, the government has resisted the cure while exacerbating the disease. In the process, we have turned just about all forms of debt into government debt, and have blown up another bubble, this time in Treasury bonds.

Unfortunately, this bubble threatens to dwarf all preceding asset bubbles. Its eventual bursting, which will cause consumer prices and interest rates to soar, will have even more devastating effects on the economy than the dot-com and housing bubbles combined.

But there is time to stop the train before it heads off the cliff. We need leaders who have the courage to be honest with voters, and voters who have the strength to accept the hard work of economic renewal.

For years we have been living beyond our means, and we must summon the resolve to finally live within them. If we can do that, and allow free market forces to operate unhindered, we can rebalance our economy and set the stage for a real expansion.

However, if we choose to put our faith in debt, the printing press, and the promise of pain-free government solutions, we will all be fishing without a net.

ACKNOWLEDGMENTS

The central allegorical model of this book is borrowed from
How an Economy Grows and Why It Doesn't, published in
1985, by Irwin A. Schiff, who generously bequeathed the idea
to his offspring.

The authors also wish to thank the contributions of Brendan
Leach who was able to illustrate quickly and creatively and
give visual dimension to our sense of humor; and the staff
at John Wiley & Sons, particularly Kelly O'Connor, whose
help was vital in putting this material together in a coherent
and entertaining package. We also would like to thank
Mike Finger at Euro Pacific Capital who provided much
philosophical and aesthetic feedback. Lastly we should thank
all of those who have supported Irwin over the years with their
thoughts and letters. It means a lot to him.

ABOUT THE AUTHORS

PETER D. SCHIFF is the popular author of the bestselling books *Crash Proof* and *The Little Book of Bull Moves in Bear Markets*, both published by John Wiley & Sons. He is a seasoned Wall Street prognosticator known for predicting the economic crisis of 2008. Schiff began his career at Shearson Lehman and joined Euro Pacific Capital—a broker-dealer with expertise in foreign markets and securities—in 1996, becoming president of the firm in 2000. He is frequently quoted in major publications such as the *Wall Street Journal*, *Barron's*, the *Financial Times*, and the *New York Times*, and has been on Squawk Box, Closing Bell, Fox News, and other programs. In 2009, he announced his candidacy for the U.S. Senate in his Home state of Connecticut. He lives in Weston, CT with his wife Martha and his son Spencer. For more, visit Peter Schiff's official book site at www.peterschiffonline.com.

ANDREW J. SCHIFF is the Communications Director of Euro Pacific Capital and long-time spokesperson and writer for the firm. An expert in media relations and financial communications, Andrew has spoken at numerous conferences and has appeared on television where he has helped articulate the themes of free market capitalism and limited government. He lives in Brooklyn, NY with his wife Paxton and their two children, Ethan and Eliza. In his spare time he reads history, looks at architecture, and plays the mandolin.

ABOUT THE ILLUSTRATOR

BRENDAN LEACH is a New York City based illustrator and comic's creator whose work has been published in *Time Out New York, Time Out New York Kids, The L magazine,* SVA *Visual Arts Journal, Paracinema Magazine, Smoke Signal,* and *Rabid Rabbit.* He received a master's degree from the School of Visual Arts in New York City. His work can be found at iknowashortcut.com. He lives in Brooklyn, New York.